The Renewal Era
# Cubs

The Renewal Era

# Cubs

1985-1990

Eddie Gold and Art Ahrens

Bonus Books, Inc., Chicago

94  93  92  91  90                              5  4  3  2  1

Library of Congress Catalog Number:
90-80680

International Standard Book Number:
0-929387-13-9

**Bonus Books, Inc.**
160 East Illinois Street
Chicago, Illinois 60611

*Printed in the United States of America*

# Contents

♦

v

# Introduction

## From the Green Machine to the Boys of Zimmer (1985–1989)

Following the 1984 division championship, the Cubs future looked bright, despite the heartbreaking loss in the playoffs. In early 1985, it appeared that the Cubs would continue as contenders, winning 34 of their first 53 games. But a wave of injuries hit the team and it was all downhill thereafter. Bobby Dernier, Gary Matthews, Rick Sutcliffe, Dennis Eckersley, Steve Trout, Scott Sanderson, and Dick Ruthven all spent time on the disabled list, while Jody Davis missed considerable action because of a virus. When the Cubs lost 13 straight (tying a club record) they were out of the race that quickly.

With the entire starting staff sidelined, Dallas Green had to reach into the farm system, only to find that it was barren of quality arms. The Cubs skidded to fifth but eventually regained fourth when the Phillies went into a tailspin. The only players who equaled or exceeded their 1984 output were Sandberg and Keith Moreland. As Larry Bowa was being phased out, Shawon Dunston began taking over the shortstop duties. He displayed fine potential, but a lack of consistency plagued him for a long time.

The Cubs continued to decline in 1986, as Jim

♦

Frey's head rolled and Gene Michael became the new manager.

With the Cubs on their way to fifth place, the half-crippled pitching staff went from bad to worse. For the first time in their history, the Cubs did not have a single pitcher who was able to win ten games. Sutcliffe, the ace of 1984, had fallen to 5–14. Even the previously dependable Lee Smith was beginning to display a disturbing tendency to get shelled in pressure situations. Dunston, in his first full season, led all NL shortstops in putouts, assists, double plays . . . and errors.

Shortly before the start of the 1987 season, the Cubs bolstered their withering offense by signing veteran outfielder Andre Dawson via free agency— and for a bargain basement price by today's standards.

It was Dallas Green's last major coup. With Dawson topping the league in homers and RBI en route to an MVP season, the Cubs were again an exciting team, if not a winning one. Led by Andre, Chicago smashed 209 home runs, to lead the league and shatter the old Cub record set back in 1958. However, the fact that the majors in general witnessed a sharp increase in homer output led many to believe that the ball had been "juiced up."

Even Dawson's heroics and a comeback year for Sutcliffe could not prevent the Cubs from falling to last in their division. They were last in the league in stolen bases and next to last in team ERA. For the third time in five years, the Cubs manager did not last the season. With 25 games left, Green fired Michael and named Frank Lucchesi as yet another interim manager.

Green was soon history himself. Shortly after the end of the campaign, he announced his resignation from the Cub organization. Many suspected that he was pressured out. Ironically, he was replaced as general manager by one of the men he had fired, Jim

Frey. Frey, in turn, named his old comrade Don
Zimmer as field boss.

One of their first deals was to trade Lee Smith to
the Red Sox for pitchers Al Nipper and Calvin Schiraldi—leaving only Davis, Durham, Sandberg, Sanderson and Sutcliffe from 1984. Although many felt
that Smith's best years were behind him, it was
equally apparent that the Cubs could have gotten
more in return by driving a harder bargain.

For the Cubs, the 1988 season was one of promise, disappointment, and even history-making. With
their copyrighted good first half, they placed six
players on the All-Star team, their most since 1936.
Thereafter, the team declined to finish fourth, eight
games below .500. The primary reasons for the Cubs'
demise were a lack of clutch hitting and a totally
ineffective bullpen led by Goose Gossage, a once
fine reliever who was now over the hill. Home run
production plummeted to 113, barely half of the
1987 total.

There were positive developments also. Rookie
Mark Grace caught on immediately at first base,
sending Durham to Cincinnati. Damon Berryhill, another rookie, began to supplant Davis behind the
plate and did so well that by September, Davis was
gone, too. Twenty-two-year-old Greg Maddux won 18
games, and sophomore Rafael Palmeiro hit for an
impressive average, but with little power. After decades of blight, the Cubs' farm system was finally
beginning to produce good crops.

After months of negotiations between the Chicago City Council, the Illinois State Legislature and
neighborhood pressure groups, night baseball finally
became a reality at Wrigley Field on Aug. 8, 1988.
However, with the Cubs leading the Phillies, 3–1, in
the bottom of the fourth, a torrential downpour and a
two hour delay caused the affair to be cancelled
because of rain. Somehow, it was fitting. The follow-

ing evening, in the first night game that counted, the Cubs took the Mets, 6–4.

Finally, on Sept. 30, 1988, President Ronald Reagan became the first chief executive to attend a Cub game while in office since William Howard Taft in 1909. A former sportscaster himself, the president briefly joined Harry Caray in the radio booth to help with the play-by-play. Unfortunately, the Pirates put the damper on the affair by edging the Cubs, 10–9, in 10 innings. The Cubs had lost one for the Gipper.

During the winter, the Cubs began preparing for the new year by making another controversial trade. Rafael Palmeiro and pitchers Jamie Moyer and Drew Hall were swapped to Texas for pitchers Mitch Williams, Paul Kilgus and Steve Wilson, infielders Curt Wilkerson and Luis Benetiz, and outfielder Pablo Delgado. By obtaining this assemblage of unknown quantities, the Cubs appeared to be getting swindled, as usual.

That was the way it still looked at the close of a miserable spring training. The overall prognosis was that the Cubs would finish fifth. Said Steve Wulf of *Sports Illustrated,* "The Cubs, who haven't won a world championship since 1908, have had only one winning season since 1972. You can be certain this will not be their second." Frey and Zimmer would later concede that they were only hoping the team would be good enough to break even.

With the season underway, the Cubs defied the experts by pulling off one miracle after another. Lefty reliever Mitch Williams gave fans cardiac arrest with his erratic control and unorthodox delivery, but got the job done. Mike Bielecki, who had previously won only 12 games in his entire career, came through with 18 wins. Outfielders Jerome Walton and Dwight Smith, neither of whom had played beyond Class AA ball, responded with outstanding rookie seasons.

After four seasons of inconsistent promise,

♦

Shawon Dunston finally became a genuine major leaguer at the plate as well as in the field. Maddux won 19 and Sutcliffe 16. Sandberg had a fine season while Grace did not fall victim to the proverbial sophomore jinx. Journeyman outfielder Lloyd Mc-Clendon provided added bench strength while Luis Salazar, obtained from San Diego late in the year to help the slumping Vance Law at third base, put forth a hot bat.

Although the 1989 Cubs flirted with first place during the early months of the season, there was still a sense of impending doom among their fans, who waited for the inevitable August or September collapse. But this time, the swoon did not come as the "Boys of Zimmer" took the lead for keeps on August 7. When the Cubs rallied to defeat the Astros, 10–9, on August 29, after spotting them a 9–0 lead, many a non-believer was converted. Dwight Smith remarked, "It's a message this club is for real."

The Cubs clinched the NL East crown on September 26 with a 3–2 victory over the Expos at Montreal. Appropriately, Mitch Williams fanned Mike Fitzgerald with the tying run on third base with two out in the bottom of the ninth to preserve the win for Maddux. The Cubs had won their division despite sub-par years from Andre Dawson and Vance Law, losing Damon Berryhill to the disabled list, not having a solid fourth starter, and not having at least one player with 80 or more RBI. A city record 2,491,942 paid their way into ancient Wrigley Field in its 75th anniversary season.

In the meantime, the Giants had outlasted the Padres in the West, with home run power that the Cubs could not match. The Cubs entered the playoffs as underdogs and came out the same way, bowing to San Francisco in five games. The power punch of Will Clark, Kevin Mitchell and Matt Williams utterly demolished the Cub pitching staff. Cub fans could only

♦

appreciate game two, a 9–5 Cub victory at Wrigley Field. Nevertheless, their demise was hardly like the trauma of 1984. It was simply a case of a fine team getting beat by a better one.

As the 1990 season approaches, the Cubs' situation is one of guarded optimism. They won the division title in spite of some glaring weaknesses. On the other hand, they have a team largely composed of young players whose best years should be ahead of them. Hopefully, their 1989 heroics will signify the renewal of a winning tradition.

# 1989

# The Boys of Zimmer

B. May 26, 1931, Cleveland, Ohio   BL TL   5'9"   170 lbs.

## JIM FREY

Courtesy of Chicago Cubs

Great Gottfried. This small-Frey resembles Harry Truman. And like Harry, he really raised some hell. The bespectacled, balding, banty battler helped turn the bumbling, loveable Cubbies into a winner in one season.

◆
1

James Gottfried Frey was undoubtedly the best Cubs' manager since the reign of Leo Durocher. And Frey took the Cubs further than the Lip did in six stormy seasons.

The Ohio-born Frey is a tried and true Buckeye, born in Cleveland, reared in Cincinnati, and educated in Columbus (at Ohio State). A graduate of Cincy's Western Hills High, Frey spent 14 seasons in the bush leagues, never sipping a drop of big league coffee.

His record reads like a railroad timetable with whistle stops in Evansville, Paducah, Hartford, Jacksonville, Toledo, Atlanta, Austin, Fort Worth, Tulsa, Omaha, Rochester, Buffalo, and Columbus from 1950 through 1963.

Although the left-handed hitting outfielder boasted a .302 batting average, he bounced from one big league organization to another. At times he was the property of the Braves, Dodgers, Cardinals, and Pirates.

Frey enjoyed perhaps his finest season in 1957 with Tulsa, topping the Texas League with a .336 average and winning the Most Valuable Player Award. In addition, he led with 102 runs scored, 198 hits, 294 total bases, 50 doubles, 11 triples, and tied for the lead in stolen bases with 21.

As a result, he was invited to the Cardinals' spring training camp in St. Petersburg, Florida, in 1958. Frey was told by manager Fred Hutchinson that he beat out the promising Curt Flood for the center field job, but he hurt his arm and his chance was gone forever.

"I was a singles hitter," revealed Frey. "Big, fat guys used to beat me out all the time because they hit home runs. I would never say I would have been a good major leaguer. I would have been one of those guys on the fringe."

Frey started his managerial career at the bottom, spending two uneventful years at Bluefield of the

♦

Appalachian League. His teams finished fourth and fifth in 1963 and 1964. He then joined the Baltimore organization as a scout, before serving a decade under Earl Weaver as a coach.

"I never thought about managing," said the soft-spoken Frey. "I was proud to be a major league coach."

Meanwhile, Kansas City dumped popular manager Whitey Herzog because the Royals failed three times to beat out the New York Yankees in the American League playoffs. Frey answered the call to manage the Royals in 1980.

Kansas City won 97 and lost 65, winning the AL West by 14 games and then swept the hated Yankees in three games, highlighted by George Brett's towering three-run homer off Goose Gossage, turning a 2–1 deficit to a 4–2 pennant clincher.

Frey clashed head-on with the Phillies, managed by Dallas Green, in the World Series and lost in six games. Then Frey faced further problems. He set up a stringent dress code and incurred the wrath of a few casually clothed players, who didn't meet his penchant for sartorial splendor.

He gave outfielder Willie Wilson a dressing down for not wearing a sport jacket as the Royals prepared for a road trip. Wilson left in a huff. In addition, the Royals' record turned ragged during the strike-shortened 1981 season.

The team record was 30–41 when Frey was replaced by Dick Howser on August 31. Jim then joined the New York Mets in 1982 as coach and batting instructor. His prize pupil was Darryl Strawberry, the peaches and cream of the rookie crop of 1983.

Frey was next summoned to Chicago by Dallas Green for his second shot as a big league pilot. He became the Cubs' 36th manager with the announcement on Oct. 6, 1983. "I like the way he looks you square in the eye," said Green. Dallas must've been seated at the time because he stands 6'6" to Frey's 5'9".

♦

Although Jimmy inherited a mediocre ballclub, the Cubs clinched the National League East title. Frey thus became the first manager in major league history to guide teams in both leagues to divisional championships his first season at the helm.

On the final day of the 1984 regular season, after the Cubs rallied for two runs in the ninth inning to edge the Cardinals 2–1, Frey marched his entire ballclub onto the field and doffed his cap to the Chicago fans. Despite their failure to punish the Padres in the playoffs, Frey was the popular choice as National League Manager of the Year.

Frey saw his entire 1985 starting staff disintegrate before his eyes. Fresh troops brought in from the bushes were not refreshing. The team slid from first to fourth and finished with a 77–84 record. The next season Frey went from fried to fired.

The Cubs were 23–33 when he was dismissed by Dallas. Frey stuck around until he was replaced by "The Stick," Gene Michael, in June 1986. At least Frey had a winning record (196–182), a rarity for a Cubs manager.

But he bounced back as a broadcaster, spending the 1987 season as a color commentator on WGN radio. Meanwhile, the Cub organization was seeking someone low-keyed. They low-bridged Dallas Green, who went with a loud splash.

Green's job was handed to Frey. His title was executive vice-president, baseball operations. He hired his old buddy Don Zimmer as manager. Frey then satisfied the Cub brass by unloading fading veterans and slicing the salary structure.

Gone from the roster were Leon Durham, Lee Smith, Keith Moreland, and Jody Davis, among others. Perhaps his best deal drew scant ink in the press. It involved two guys named Mike and was consummated Mar. 31, 1988. Frey sent left-hander Mike Curtis to the Pirates for right-hander Mike Bielecki.

◆

But the Cubs faded to fifth with a 77–85 record in 1988. Frey's main task was to rebuild the pitching staff. He was roasted at the outset for trading popular outfielder Rafael Palmeiro to Texas for three pitchers and toasted as the team somehow wound up first in the NL East.

After watching the Cubs get drubbed by the Giants in the 1989 Championship playoffs, Frey knows what the team needs to repeat in 1990—power, pitching, and pluck.

Frey failed to fetch fancy-priced free agents the past winter. Cub fans are growing restless and it's all up to Frey for the flag to fly over Wrigley Field.

**B. Jan. 17, 1931, Cincinnati, Ohio   BR TR   5′9″   185 lbs.**

# DON ZIMMER

Courtesy of Chicago Cubs

Cub managers have run the gamut from Anson to Zimmer. Adrian Constantine Anson was usually called Cap, but in his later days was called Pop. Donald William Zimmer is called simply Popeye.

Managing the Cubs is enough to tear out your heart or your hair or both. Zimmer has a lot of heart but no hair.

The portly pilot has been part of baseball for more than 40 years as a player, a coach, a manager, and a groom. That's right, a groom. On Aug. 14, 1951, Don and his wife Jean were married at home plate in Elmira, N.Y. Ever since, they've been happily married —to each other and to baseball.

His career started two years earlier. He played with Cambridge of the Eastern Shore League. Zim got hot at Hornell (1950), where he batted .315 with 23 homers, 122 RBI, and 63 stolen bases.

Two things kept the Cincinnati Kid from making it to the Dodgers. One was injuries and the other was a chap named Pee Wee Reese, who patrolled shortstop for the Brooklyn Dodgers.

In 1953, while playing for St. Paul, Zimmer was struck in the head by a pitch thrown by Columbus' Jim Kirk. And in 1956 while playing for Brooklyn, Don was struck in the face by a pitch from Cincy's Hal Jeffcoat, a former Cub outfielder.

Zimmer was batting .300 at the time of both injuries. A plate was inserted in Popeye's bald pate and he continued his playing career.

Zimmer tripled off the Phillies' Curt Simmons in his first big league at-bat in 1954, but all he found in Brooklyn was futility as a utility infielder.

It wasn't until the Dodgers went cross-country to Los Angeles in 1958 that Don became a semi-regular. Reese was reaching the end of the road and the squat Zimmer batted .260 with 17 homers and 60 RBI.

But Zim was only a stopgap shortstop. A new morning glory named Maurice Morning Wills was waiting in the wings. Wills had faster wheels than Don and stole the job with his many base thefts.

♦

The Dodgers won the National League pennant in 1959 and downed the Chicago White Sox in six games in the World Series. And by the time 1960 rolled around Zimmer wound up in a Cubs uniform.

He was traded to the Cubs for pitcher Ron Perranoski, infielder John Goryl, outfielder Lee Handley and a reported $25,000 on April 8, 1960. It was another of those one-sided Cub deals. Perranoski stepped in with the Dodgers to become the premier left-handed reliever in the league.

But Zimmer paid immediate dividends as a Cub. In his first time at bat he homered off Dodgers ace right-hander Don Drysdale and drew a standing ovation before 67,500 fans at the L.A. Coliseum. It was the largest crowd ever to watch a Cubs game.

Zimmer continued to see action as a Cub, but again not at shortstop. Ernie Banks was a fixture there, and Ron Santo eventually beat out Don at third base. So Zim settled down at second base.

In his two seasons as a Cub, Zimmer batted .254 with 19 homers and 75 RBI in 260 games. The NL expanded to ten teams in 1962 and Zimmer was selected by the New York Mets in the draft on Oct. 10, 1961.

Zimmer thus was an original Met, patrolling third base for manager Casey Stengel. The New Yorkers won 40 and lost 120 and finished a distant 10th, 60½ games out of first place.

He also played for the Reds, went back to the Dodgers, and eventually wound up in Washington. And in his first trip to the plate as a Senator, Zimmer homered. Then he had a yen to play in Japan, spending the 1966 season with the Toei Flyers.

Zimmer finally hung up his spikes after being shuffled off to Buffalo in 1967. In a dozen big league seasons, Zimmer spanked 91 homers with 352 RBI, and a lukewarm .235 average.

By pounding the pines, Zimmer picked up

◆

enough baseball savvy to find a spot as a coach. He served as second banana with the Expos, Padres, Red Sox, Yankees, Cubs, and Giants.

Zim started his managerial career with San Diego, replacing Preston Gomez in April 1972. His Padres were powerless and pitch-poor and posted 54–88 and 60–102 records.

Zimmer had better success in Boston, directing the Red Sox for five seasons from 1976 to 1980. In that time, he compiled a 411–304 mark. But Zimmer had his problems with some players, who dubbed him the "Gerbil."

The ruddy-cheeked round man then bounced to Texas in 1981 and led the Rangers to a tepid 95–116 record in parts of two long, hot seasons. When Jim Frey was named Cubs manager in 1984, his first move was to install Zimmer as third base coach. Frey and Zimmer grew up together in Cincinnati. They attended Western Hills High School and played on the same baseball and basketball teams. Could you imagine Zimmer in basketball togs?

Frey was fired as Cubs manager midway through the 1986 season, but came back as color commentator on radio. When he became general manager in 1988, his selection of Zimmer as manager was a foregone conclusion.

Don was named the Cubs' 40th manager on Nov. 20, 1987. He is the 15th former Cub player to manage the team.

Many detractors called Zimmer's promotion part of the buddy or "good, ol' boys system." But, at least there was some animation in Zimmer compared to the departed, lifeless Gene Michael.

Zimmer's first season as boss was more mild than wild. The Cubs finished fourth in the NL East with a 77–85 record. But Zimmer became a resident genius in 1989.

With Zimmer's penchant for hunches, the Cubs

♦

had 33 comeback victories, including 20 after July 20. They won 16 games in their final at-bat, including 11 after July 11.

All this led to a 93–69 mark and the clinching of the NL East title after a long stretch battle with the Cardinals, Mets, and Expos. But in the NL Championship series against the Giants, the Cinderella team no longer had a ball.

Most of Zimmer's maneuvers backfired. The Giants won four of five games to end the Cub season. Some say the team choked. But they fail to mention the Giants just had too much Will-power from the bat of Will Clark.

B. June 21, 1956, Independence, Mo.   BL TR   6'7"   220 lbs.

# RICK SUTCLIFFE

Courtesy of Chicago Cubs

Color the beard red. Paint his currency green. And pencil him in Cubbie blue for the next five years.

♦

Never in the 109-year history of the Cubs has a player made such an impact in such a short span as Rick Sutcliffe, a gentle giant of a pitcher. At $9.5 million he is the highest-paid player in team history —more than Tinker-to-Evers-to-Chance, Hack Wilson, Gabby Hartnett, Ernie Banks, and Moe Thacker earned in their collective careers.

The Sutcliffe saga began on June 13, 1984. The Cubs gambled away their future by shipping outfielders Mel Hall and Joe Carter, plus pitchers Don Schulze and Darryl Banks to the Cleveland Indians for catcher Ron Hassey, pitcher George Frazier, and the Big Guy.

During the Cubs' pennant-winning season of 1984, Sutcliffe became the first pitcher since Hank Borowy to reach 20 victories in a season in both leagues.

His 20–6 combined record earned him the NL Cy Young Award, joining Fergie Jenkins (1971) and reliever Bruce Sutter (1979) among the Cubs' previous winners.

Richard Lee Sutcliffe was born in Independence, Missouri, the son of sprint-car driver Dick Sutcliffe, who was known on the circuit as "Mr. Excitement." His parents were divorced when Rick was 10. He and his brother and sister were raised by their maternal grandparents, Bill and Alice Yearout.

Sutcliffe was rated All-State in baseball, football, and track when he was selected by the Los Angeles Dodgers in the first round (21st player) of the free agent draft on June 5, 1974. It was reported he signed for an $80,000 bonus.

Former Cub shortstop Lennie Merullo, now a big league scout, recalls seeing Sutcliffe perform with Waterbury of the Eastern League in 1976. "Sutcliffe was more of a sidearmer then, like Ewell Blackwell, observed Merullo. "He always seemed to have a smile on his face. Now, he has that red beard and appears

♦

meaner. He really stares them down. That sinker and slider were tough to hit, even then."

Sutcliffe came up to the Dodgers to stick in 1979 and was named National League Rookie of the Year with a 17–10 record. In addition, he proved handy with the bat, driving in 17 runs and averaging .247. Ironically, Sutcliffe encountered the most trouble with the lowly Cubs, losing three of four contests. He also fell victim to the sophomore jinx in 1980 as his record plummeted to 3–9.

Generally affable, cheerful, and talkative, Sutcliffe became an ogre during the strike-shortened 1981 season. He spent much of the time on the disabled list, had pitched only 47 innings and was 2–2 when he was scratched from the 25-player roster for the playoffs and World Series.

That set off his fuse and the fireworks began. Rick stormed into Dodger manager Tom Lasorda's office, knocked everything off his desk, then overturned the desk. With Lasorda, that performance meant Rick wouldn't last very long with the Dodgers.

He was exiled to the Indians on Dec. 9, 1981, going with second baseman Jack Perconte for pitcher Larry White, outfielder Jorge Orta, and catcher Jack Fimple.

At Cleveland Sutcliffe pitched even better than his record indicated. Although he was 14–8, Rick was the league's earned run average leader at 2.96. Sutcliffe should have been a 20-game winner in 1983, but had to settle for 17–11. On five occasions that Sutcliffe pitched, the Indians were shut out.

Sutcliffe was on the final year of his $900,000 per season contract, so it was a known fact that the Indians were ready to peddle him. Dallas Green took that chance, knowing Rick would be a megabucks free agent at the conclusion of the 1984 season. Sutcliffe with his agent, Barry Axelrod, filed for free agency on Oct. 19, 1984.

◆

Then the bidding wars began. Salvos were fired from across the nation, from Atlanta, to Kansas City, to San Diego, and back to Chicago. It was down to the Braves, Royals, Padres, and Cubs for Sutcliffe's services.

Ted Turner of the Braves was a charmer. He had just lured relief ace Bruce Sutter from the St. Louis Cardinals for a contract that reportedly extended to the 21st century.

Turner, with an unlimited cable-TV bankroll, wanted Rick to join Sutter, plus sluggers Dale Murphy and Bob Horner in his gala galaxy. The Royals were relying on the hometown aspect, while the Padres were offering the sun, sea, surf of San Diego, plus the friendship of teammates Steve Garvey and Goose Gossage.

The weeks rolled by. Finally, on Friday, December 14, a decision was reached. Sutcliffe would remain in Chicago. Rick met the media at Wrigley Field and expressed his loyalty to the Cubs. Green raised his right arm in triumph. And the Tribune Company shelled out over $9.5 million for five years.

As the most wanted man since Dillinger, Rick stepped to the podium and smiled. Then he declared, "I owe it to Chicago. Call it a sense of loyalty or whatever you want to call it, but something happened the three and a half months I was here. It was the fans, the players, the city. We got farther than any Cub team in years, . . . but we didn't get far enough."

Although the Dodgers won the World Series in 1981 and Sutcliffe earned a series ring, it has a hollow ring. Rick doesn't wear it. He wants to be fitted with a Chicago Cubs ring.

Following a 16–1 season, what can a pitcher do for an encore? Sutcliffe took his five-year, mega-bucks contract and had several roller-coaster seasons. There were many millstones and milestones along the bumpy ride.

♦

On the plus side, the Red Baron struck out his 1,000th batter, notched his 100th victory and even became the first Cub pitcher to steal home since the heyday of Hippo Vaughn in 1919. But in reality, Sutcliffe was barely over the .500 mark with a 60–57 record.

The 1985 season was a disaster. His record read more like a hospital chart. Sutcliffe was hampered by a series of injuries that put him on the disabled list three times. He was rolling along with a 5–3 record and a 2.11 earned run average before tearing his left hamstring on May 19.

Sutcliffe returned to the mound, June 7, amidst much joy, and blanked the Pirates 1–0. But that was short-lived. He went on the DL a second time with a strained left abductor muscle, July 8. A right shoulder injury ended his season on July 29.

And 1986 was worse. This time he encountered more tough luck than injuries. He struggled through a 5–14 season, that included an eight-game losing streak. He was the victim of an anemic Cub attack. The team scored 23 runs in his 14 losses.

But Rick bounced back to win the comeback award in 1987. In fact, he led the NL in victories with 18 and came within two votes of the Cy Young Award. He was edged by bullpen artist Steve Bedrosian of the Phillies. Although his pitching log read 18–10, Sutcliffe could have won a half-dozen more games if not for shoddy support in the bullpen.

During that season Sutcliffe fanned Willie McGee of the Cardinals for his 1,000th strikeout June 13 in St. Louis. And he won his 100th big league game July 22 in San Diego.

Then it was back to adversity in 1988. Despite a career-high 12 complete games, Sutcliffe could only maintain a 13–14 record. This time the Cubs tallied only 18 runs in his 14 losses.

Sutcliffe did have some fun along the way. After

♦

winning the Cubs home opener, 6–0 against the Pirates, it was revealed that Rick hurled six straight home openers, two with the Indians and four with the Cubs for a 4–2 mark.

In a July 29 triumph over the Phillies, he was credited with stealing home as part of a double-steal with Mitch Webster. Imagine a 6'7" athlete sliding home in a cloud of dust.

The red-bearded Sutcliffe was now 33 and the graybeard of a youthful Cub staff in 1989. He lost a lot of zing in his fastball and had shoulder problems, but came through with a clutch 16–11 record as the Cubs won the NL East title.

Many of Rick's victories came in timely situations, especially during the early part of the season. His fastball was humming on April 9, as he fanned 11 Pirates en route to an 8–3 triumph. Nine days later, he beat the Phillies 5–3 to extend the Cubs' winning streak to seven games. On June 17, his 3–2 edging of Montreal put the Cubs back in first place and ignited a five-game winning streak. He wrapped up the same streak with an 8–0 whitewashing of the Pirates on June 22. On August 17, Sutcliffe's 3–2 victory over the Reds pushed the Cubs' lead up to 4½ games, the highest it had been all season up to that point. Obviously, Rick enjoyed a satisfying year.

Richard Lee Sutcliffe won many cliff-hangers on the mound, but will also be remembered for his ready smile and off the field for his humanitarian services in Chicago. Going into the 1990s, Sutcliffe boasts a 76–58 mark in Cub flannels.

**B. April 14, 1966, San Angelo, Tex.   BR TR   6'0"   150 lbs.**

# GREG MADDUX

Courtesy of Chicago Cubs

A lightweight pitcher who has developed into a heavy-weight champ on the mound, Greg Maddux appears to be the key to future Cub hopes in starting pitching. Time will determine if he becomes the Fergie Jenkins of the 1990s. So far he is off to an impressive start. Despite his youth, he has been the ace of the Cub staff for the last two years.

The Cubs signed Maddux in the second round of the June 1984 draft, coinciding with his graduation from Valley High School in Las Vegas. Then, he moved up the minor league ladder from Pikeville of the Appalachian League to Peoria of the Midwest League to Pittsfield of the Eastern League to Iowa of the American Association. Over these three years, his record was fairly good, but hardly spectacular by minor league standards.

Nevertheless, his 14–4 mark in 1986 (split between Pittsfield and Iowa) earned him an advancement to the parent club. With a pitching staff that had

♦

been ineffective all season, it was figured that Maddux could not do any worse.

The Cubs were right. Maddux did no worse than the rest of the pitching corps. He did no better either. He finished at 2–4 with a not too skimpy 5.52 ERA. In 1987, it was more of the same. Batters battered Greg for a 5.61 ERA en route to a 6–14 log. In short, he looked like a typical Cub prospect. Even so, on July 1 he pitched his first major league shutout and complete game, a four-hit, 1–0 sparkler over the Expos at Montreal. In so doing, he became the youngest Cub pitcher to go the distance since Ken Holtzman 21 years prior.

But one good outing does not make a career, so there were few who nurtured great expectations for Maddux when 1988 came around. When he tossed a three-hit, 3–0 gem over Atlanta on April 6, it brought more ho-hums than cheers. When he finished the month with a 4–1 mark and a 2.20 ERA, however, fans and scribes began to take notice.

On June 1, Greg took over the league lead with nine wins, hurling a 6–3 complete-game triumph over the Reds. By June 18, he had become the NL's first 12-game winner, after defeating the Expos, 3–0. Maddux finished 5–0 with a 2.22 ERA for June, to earn the NL Pitcher of the Month honors. By now, the whole baseball world had its eyes on the 22-year-old phenom.

On July 10, Maddux pitched the Cubs to a 4–2 win over the Padres at San Diego, for his ninth straight win. The victory left him at 15–3 (2.14 ERA) at the All-Star break. Greg was one of six Cubs named to the All-Star squad, but did not see action.

At this point, Maddux looked like a cinch to win at least 20 games, but such was not to be. Although he claimed he did not feel worn out, Greg pitched as if he were, as his second half was a 3–5 washout. That the Cubs missed his early season effectiveness was obvi-

◆

ous. From a high water mark of 44–36 on July 4, they finished at 77–85. Regardless, Greg's 18 wins were tied for fifth in the NL. He became the first Cub hurler to defeat every league team at least once since Fergie Jenkins in 1971.

In early 1989, Maddux was still snake-bitten. He lost five of his first six decisions as his ERA soared. Greg slowly picked up the pieces, climbing to 8–7 by All-Star time.

By the second half of 1989, Greg was again looking like the Maddux of early 1988. He won five in a row from July 23 through August 11. To say that he won some key games in the stretch run would be an understatement. On August 7, his 5–2 distance job over the Expos gave the Cubs sole possession of first place in the NL East for the first time since June 24— a lead they would never relinquish.

But the Cubs' race to the top of their division was not without its nail-biting moments. By September 21, the Cubs had lost four out of their last five when Maddux was called upon to be the stopper. He performed the role in grand fashion, slamming the door on the Phillies, 9–1, to rebuild the first place lead to four games.

On September 26, the Cubs were in Montreal for a night game, needing one victory to clinch the NL East title. Again, Maddux was on the mound. After nursing a 3–2 lead for 8⅓ innings, Greg needed relief help from Mitch Williams to preserve the victory. Williams did what he is paid to do, and the Cubs' magic number was at last reduced to zero. For Maddux, it was his final appearance of the regular season. He finished with a 19–12 record and a 2.95 ERA. Hoping to save his arm for the playoffs, Maddux and manager Don Zimmer mutually agreed that he would skip his last turn in the rotation, thereby sacrificing a potential 20-win season. To the soft-spoken Maddux, it was no big thing.

◆

Unfortunately, the Maddux magic disappeared in the league championship series, as he was shelled in both his starts. In fairness, the rest of the Cub staff fared little better, but neither Greg nor the Cubs had anything to be ashamed of. Among starting pitchers, Maddux was the main reason they went as far as they did.

As the 1990 season opens, Greg's record stands at 45–38. Over the past two seasons, only Dave Stewart of Oakland and Orel Hershiser of Los Angeles have won more games.

B. Nov. 7, 1964, Santa Ana, Ca.   BL TL   6'4"   200 lbs.

# MITCH WILLIAMS

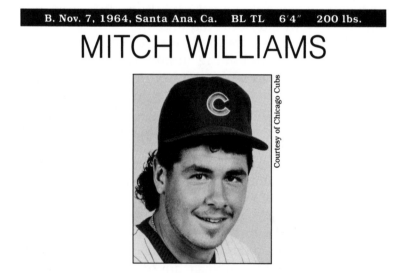

Courtesy of Chicago Cubs

The day was April 4, 1989; the season opener at Wrigley Field. Rick Sutcliffe had held the Phillies at bay but was running out of gas by the eighth inning. With one out, Don Zimmer brought in his new re-

♦

liever, Mitch Williams, heretofore unseen in the National League. With his questionable control and unorthodox delivery, Williams looked as if he would fall off the mound after every pitch.

Despite two walks and a balk, Williams managed to get through the inning without squandering the lead. However, when he gave up three singles to open the ninth, Cub fans at the park, at home, and at taverns were groaning, this is what we traded Palmeiro for?

But when he struck out Cub-killer Mike Schmidt, Chris James and Mike Ryal to preserve a 5–4 Cub victory, the crowd breathed a sigh of relief. The stage was set for an exciting but nerve-racking season.

During his four and a fraction years in the farm systems of San Diego and Texas, Williams' statistics were far from impressive. Nevertheless, the Rangers brought him up in 1986. Mitch hardly looked like a world beater but he did fairly well, posting 8–6 records in his first two seasons. In 1988, he increased his save count to 18, but his record dropped to 2–7 as his ERA ballooned to 4.63.

On Dec. 5, 1988, the Cubs traded Rafael Palmeiro, Jamie Moyer, and Drew Hall to the Rangers for Williams, Paul Kilgus, Steve Wilson, Curt Wilkerson, Luis Benetiz and Pablo Delgado. Although the Cubs had received six players for three, the general opinion was that it was another Brock for Broglio deal.

When the saves—and Cub victories—began to pile up, the fans began to thaw. Quickly nicknamed "The Wild Thing," after a popular song, Williams made it an adventure whenever he pitched—and occasionally did blow save opportunities.

He had come to Chicago with the reputation of being a bit eccentric and lived up to it. Before the season had begun, he had said, "I don't pattern myself after anybody. I'm a little different. Trust me." More often than not, he could be trusted to save the game, even if he caused cardiac arrest in doing so. On April 28, he entered the game with two out in the ninth. Before even throwing his first pitch, he picked the Padres' Carmelo Martinez off second to preserve a 3–1 victory for Paul Kilgus. By June 2, he had collected 14 saves, more than any Cub reliever in 1988. By June 17, he had already set a team record for saves by a left hander with 16.

With his deadly fastball and reputation for poor control, Mitch effectively kept batters from digging in on him at the plate. Said right fielder Andre Dawson, "You never know what's going to happen when Mitch Williams is out there."

Sometimes it really was frightening. The Cubs were leading 4–2 at Pittsburgh on August 5 when Mitch entered the game in the ninth inning. As always, Williams was veering to his right as he fired his fastball to infielder Jeff King. King lined a shot that hit Williams in the left ear. Mitch fell to the ground as Don Zimmer and trainer John Fierro rushed out of the dugout. Upon recovering, The Wild Thing pleaded with Zimmer to let him stay in. The request was refused.

Mitch did not need to be hospitalized. The next day he said, "I've been hit in the head with other objects before. I was hit in the head repeatedly by my brother." On another occasion, he remarked on the heat at Wrigley Field, "Somebody turned up the heat and humidity in this town." Yogi Berra isn't the only one able to come up with such offbeat quips.

If the 1989 Cubs were a miracle team, then Williams was their definitive miracle man. On September 11, he entered with two out in the ninth and the Cubs leading the Expos, 4–3. After his first pitch, he caught Jeff Huson napping at first base, and picked him off to end the game. This led to a three game sweep of Montreal, effectively demoralizing them and eliminating the Expos from the race.

♦

Exactly one week later, the Cubs came home for another key game, this time against the Mets. In the bottom of the eighth, Mitch came to bat with the Cubs nursing a come-from-behind 7–6 lead. The Wild Thing made his first major league hit a memorable one, slugging a three run home run to put the Cubs ahead by four. The next inning, he finished the game by striking out Met powerhouse Darryl Strawberry.

By September 26, the Cubs needed but one win to clinch the NL East division championship. Greg Maddux had held the Expos to seven hits and two runs in 8⅓ innings. He left after Tom Foley opened the ninth with a single and Nelson Santovenia bunted pinch-runner Otis Nixon to second.

In came Williams, who got pinch hitter Wallace Johnson to pop up for the second out. Then Nixon stole third without a throw. Once again, the pressure was on Williams to pull the Cubs' chestnuts out of the fire.

Williams worked pinch hitter Mike Fitzgerald to a 1–2 count. But when Fitzgerald failed to check his next swing, Williams and the Cubs froze until plate umpire Dutch Rennert's right arm soared up. The Cubs had won the title, and Mitch finished the season exactly as he had begun it—throwing a third strike with the tying run on third. Said The Wild Thing, "I didn't think about anything but 'Let's get this thing over with right now.' "

His final appearance of the regular season gave Mitch 36 saves to go with his 4–4 record and 2.65 ERA. In 81⅔ innings, he fanned 67 while walking 52.

Mitch saw little action in the playoffs, mainly because the Cubs seldom had the lead. Through 1989, his record is 22–23 with 68 saves. Hopefully, he will be the ace of the Cub bullpen for years to come.

♦

**B. April 21, 1962, Dallas, Tex.   BR TR   6'2"   200 lbs.**

# LES LANCASTER

Courtesy of Chicago Cubs

Les Lancaster has more or less bounced around baseball. Sometimes he loses track of the outs in an inning
or the count on the batter. And he has slid in and out
of the Cubs doghouse. But in 1989 he helped put
them in the penthouse.

Lancaster also has a flair for the dramatic. Who
could forget his performance against the San Francisco Giants in a nationally televised game at Wrigley
Field on July 20?

The Cubs spotted the Giants a 3–0 lead, then
went down to their final out in the ninth inning before
scoring three runs in that same inning. Les entered
the scene in the 11th inning and gave them more
thrills.

The Giants put a man on third in the top of the
inning, but couldn't score. Then with two gone in the
bottom of the inning, Curt Wilkerson singled. The
Cubs were shy on manpower, so Lancaster had to
supply his own power at bat.

♦

But the Giants were down to their last pitcher, Randy McCament. Lancaster promptly doubled down the left field line and Wilkerson chugged around the bases to score for a crucial 4–3 victory.

It wasn't always that glorious for Lancaster, who wasn't exactly in great demand by the big league scouts. Lester Wayne Lancaster was selected by the New York Yankees in the 24th round of the June 1981 draft.

His name came up again in 1983. This time he was grabbed by the Texas Rangers in the 39th round. He finally latched on with the Cubs June 13, 1985, as a non-drafted free agent.

The Dallas native rose quickly in the Cubs organization. In 1987 he was invited to the Cubs' spring camp as a non-roster player.

Lancaster was recalled from Iowa on June 22. He became a starter and pitched long and short relief. He posted an 8–3 record, the most by a Cub rookie since Willie Hernandez and Mike Krukow won eight each in 1977. He was even selected to *Baseball Digest*'s all-rookie team.

Then came an unkind cut in the new season. He struggled through his first few appearances before coming down with acute appendicitis and was placed on the disabled list. When the Cubs turned on the Wrigley lights on August 8, Lancaster was part of the big splash.

During a long rain-delay, the playful pitcher joined five other Cub mates in belly-flopping along the wet tarp to the delight of the rain-dampened fans. Zimmer simmered, while general manager Jim Frey fried.

It also didn't help when he broke a bone in his right foot during the dog days of August. He didn't return to the roster and finished with a 4–6 record. Lancaster didn't figure in Cub plans for 1989 and the opener found him toiling at Iowa. Luckily for him, the Cubs always seem short of pitching.

♦

Lancaster answered the call to arms June 24 and really fired away. He set a Cub record for a reliever by hurling 30.2 consecutive scoreless innings. His forte was long-distance relief.

Perhaps his most outstanding performance was in relief of the struggling Rick Sutcliffe at New York on September 4. Les started the sixth inning and pitched four shutout innings, allowing only one hit to preserve a 7–3 win over the Mets.

Lancaster's 4–2 record was enhanced by a stingy 1.32 earned run average and 8 saves. With the team thin in the starting ranks, Lancaster could move into the rotation for the start of the 1990s.

B. July 31, 1959, Baltimore, Md.   BR TR   6′3″   200 lbs.

# MIKE BIELECKI

Courtesy of Chicago Cubs

Of the many exceptional players on the 1989 Cubs, perhaps the most surprising was Mike Bielecki. A

♦
**24**

long time minor league veteran who had attracted virtually no attention during bits and pieces of five big league seasons, Bielecki was the number one nobody on the Cub staff when spring training closed. By the end of September, Mike was their second biggest winner. He compiled six more victories in his latest campaign than during his entire previous major league career.

Ten years earlier, Mike had made his professional debut with Bradenton of the Gulf Coast League. In the years that followed, he toiled for Shelby and Greenwood of the South Atlantic League, Buffalo and Lynn of the Eastern League, and Hawaii of the Pacific Coast League. His 19 victories for Hawaii in 1984 won him a chance with the Pirates late in the season.

Over the next three years, Bielecki won a not-so-grand total of 10 games for the Bucs, in between demotions to Hawaii and Vancouver. His closest thing to a full season in the majors was 1986, when he posted a 6–11 record with a 4.66 ERA in 149 innings. His baseball future looked equivalent to a prisoner's on death row. On Mar. 31, 1988, Bielecki was traded to the Cubs for pitcher Mike Curtis.

Mike won the 1988 season opener in relief—a 13-inning, 10–9 win over the Braves on April 5 at Atlanta—but that did not prevent him from being sent to the Cubs' Triple A farm club several weeks later. He came back in time to start the first official Cub home night game on August 9. He was not the pitcher of record, but the Cubs beat the Mets, 6–4, thanks to a four-run seventh inning. Briefly hospitalized with salmonella poisoning, Mike finished his Cub season at 2–2 with a 3.35 ERA.

As 1989 grew near, Bielecki's major league record stood at 12–19 with a 4.37 ERA. With his 30th birthday fast approaching, Mike appeared to be among the least likely Cub pitchers to succeed.

When the season got underway, Mike continued

♦

to perform in his quiet, unassuming manner. This time, however, he was winning ball games with regularity. On May 15, his 4–0 victory over the Braves snapped a five game Cub losing streak. From July 14 until September 3, he enjoyed six triumphs without a defeat. Winding up with a juicy 18–7 record, he led the team in winning percentage (.714) and shutouts (three). His 3.14 ERA was second to Greg Maddux among Cub starters.

Unfortunately for the Cubs, Bielecki was the only Cub starter who displayed any effectiveness against the Giants in the League Championship Series. Starting the second game, Mike was yanked with two out and two on in the fifth inning, and the Cubs up, 6–2. The Cubs held on to win, 9–5, for their only victory of the playoffs. Mike was just one out short of being the winning pitcher.

In the fifth game, Mike was nearly flawless for six innings, allowing just two hits while his teammates eked out a 1–0 lead. In the seventh, Will Clark led off with a curving line drive that right fielder Andre Dawson, after stumbling, caught up to but could not hold. He then overran the ball as Clark chugged into third base. Kevin Mitchell then sent a sacrifice fly to center, tying the game at one apiece.

That was how it stood until the last of the eighth, when Bielecki fell apart. With two outs, he walked three straight batters. Having obviously waited too long, manager Don Zimmer finally brought in Mitch Williams to face the red hot Clark. On an 0–2 count, "Will the Thrill" singled to give the Friscos a 3–1 lead. Although Chicago came back with one in the ninth, it was too little, too late. The League Championship Series and the Cubs were history.

At the end of the regular season, Mike had re-marked, "I couldn't be happier. In fact, for the first time in my baseball career, I feel secure enough about my job next summer that I'm going to stay here this

◆

winter. If it gets too cold in Chicago, I'll just go back home to Baltimore." In view of the arctic deep freeze that swept into Chicago last December, it is likely that he retreated at least temporarily. Going into 1990, Bielecki has 30 wins and 26 losses.

**B. Dec. 13, 1964, Vancouver, B.C., Can.   BL TL   6'4"   195 lbs.**

# STEVE WILSON

Courtesy of Chicago Cubs

Pitcher Steve Wilson was among the many previously unknown youngsters who helped the Cubs win a division title in 1989. Although used primarily as a middle reliever, Wilson also made some spot starts and generally rose to the occasion when the pressure was on.

In his days at University of Portland, Steve hurled two no-hitters, including a perfect game. He also pitched in the Pan American Games in 1983, and for the Canadian Olympic team in Europe in 1984.

♦

During the 1988 season, Wilson emerged as one of the stars at Double A Tulsa of the Texas League, putting together a 15–7 record with a 3.16 ERA. He also won three postseason games, helping Tulsa win the Texas League championship. Seeing brief action with the Texas Rangers, Wilson was decisionless in his first major league appearance. On Dec. 5, 1988, he was swapped to the Cubs with pitchers Mitch Williams and Paul Kilgus, infielders Curt Wilkerson and Luis Benetiz, and outfielder Pablo Delgado for outfielder Rafael Palmeiro, and pitchers Jamie Moyer and Drew Hall.

Steve was pitching in relief on April 7, 1989, when he notched his first major league victory in a 6–5 thriller over the Pirates at Wrigley Field. He continued to work out of the bullpen for the next two months.

But on June 12 Rick Sutcliffe, the scheduled starter, checked in with a sore back. Called in as an emergency starter, Wilson received credit for the win in a 10–3 victory over the Cardinals that snapped a three-game losing streak. In his next starting assignment, on August 1, he pitched the Cubs to a 4–1 win at Philadelphia.

Perhaps his best game, although a no-decision, came on September 10. Pitching on three hours' notice in place of Greg Maddux, Steve fanned ten Cardinals in five innings but was behind 1–0 when he was lifted. The Cubs went on to a 4–1 victory, as four pitchers combined for 18 strikeouts. Scott Sanderson got the win. This win rebuilt the Cubs' lead in the NL East to 2½ games. Two weeks later, Wilson won his sixth and final game of the year, allowing one run and three hits in five-plus innings as the Cubs beat the Pirates, 4–2 in the final Cub home game of the regular season. Most of the 37,000 fans would not leave until the Cubs returned to the field for a curtain call reminiscent of 1984.

◆

Steve finished with a 6–4 record, two saves, and a 4.20 ERA in 86 innings. While he has yet to prove himself on a long-term basis, he certainly came through when he was needed last season.

**B. July 22, 1956, Dearborn, Mich.  BR TR  6'5"  200 lbs.**

# SCOTT SANDERSON

Courtesy of Chicago Cubs

In his six years in a Cub uniform, Scott Sanderson was a perpetual question mark. Although an effective pitcher when he was well, Sanderson was plagued with ailments throughout his stay in Chicago.

Although born in the Detroit area, Scott spent his formative years in Northbrook, Illinois. He graduated from Glenbrook North High School. Drafted by the Royals in 1974, he opted for Vanderbilt University instead, majoring in business finance and history.

Upon entering professional ball in 1977, Sanderson moved up the ladder in little time. Debuting with

♦

West Palm Beach of the Florida State League, he went to Memphis of the Southern League the following year, then on to Denver of the American Association in midseason. By the end of 1978, Scott was with the Montreal Expos. As a rookie he was 4–2 with a 2.51 ERA in 61 innings.

During his first five years with the Expos, Scott's ERAs were always respectable, but he never fully lived up to the high hopes Montreal had for him. His victory column saw double figures only twice, with a 16–11 mark in 1980—his best to date—and a 12–12 log in 1982, when he finished strong to win six of his last seven decisions. He posted a career high 158 strikeouts that season.

Then came the disastrous 1983 season. Tearing ligaments in his right thumb in a baserunning mishap at Wrigley Field on July 4, Sanderson remained on the disabled list until September 1. He finished the year with a 6–7 record and a 4.62 ERA.

The pitching-dry, fifth-place Cubs were anxious to improve their pitching staff and willing to give Scott another chance, even if he appeared to be damaged goods. Scott, then, became a Cub on Dec. 7, 1983, in a three-team deal. The Expos acquired pitcher Gary Lucas from San Diego while the Padres soaked the Cubs for infielders Carmelo Martinez and Fritz Connally and pitcher Craig Lefferts.

In the early stages of 1984, Scott looked like he was headed for an outstanding year, winning four of his first five decisions and ranking among the league leaders in ERA. On April 28 he allowed just two hits in leading the Cubs to a 7–1 romp at Pittsburgh, facing only 28 batters.

On May 9 Scott was breezing toward a 5–0 win over the Dodgers when back spasms forced him out of the game after five innings. Although he received credit for the victory, Sanderson did not appear again

♦

until May 15. He lasted for only two batters before the spasms flared up again.

Scott rested for two weeks before pitching again on May 29 at Atlanta. He lasted just three innings before the spasms reoccurred. This time he was placed on the disabled list, spending a week in a Chicago hospital.

Reactivated on July 5, Sanderson went 5⅓ innings to beat the Giants 9–3, but saw little action thereafter, finishing with an 8–5 record and a 3.14 ERA. In his one appearance in the playoffs, he was ineffective but decisionless.

During the years that followed, Scott was just as apt to be on the disabled list as on the mound, largely because of chronic back problems. Back on the DL on Aug. 14, 1985, he remained there for the rest of the season. He came back the following year to tie Lee Smith for the club lead in wins, although the total was a paltry nine. By 1987, he was again off and on the DL. His pitching accomplishments during these years were marginal.

On April 15, 1988, Sanderson underwent surgery for a herniated disc in his lumbar spine. He was sidelined until August 23, and saw only limited action during the tail end of the year. Many had doubted that he would ever pitch again.

Scott defied the odds and made a fairly respectable comeback in 1989, winning 11 and losing 9 with a 3.94 ERA. Although it was his highest victory total in seven years, he was generally less effective during the second half of the season. Dropped from the starting rotation in early August, he won only one game thereafter—a 3–1 triumph over the Expos on September 13.

Sanderson opted for free agency over the winter, signing with the Oakland Athletics. Through 1989, his lifetime record is 98–89. As a Cub he was 42–42.

♦

**B. Feb. 12, 1966, Antioch, Calif.    BR TR    6'2"    170 lbs.**

# JEFF PICO

Courtesy of Chicago Cubs

On May 31, 1988, a 22-year-old from the Cubs' Triple A club in Iowa, who had never hurled a pitch in the majors, took the mound against the Reds. By the time the contest was over, Jeff Pico had become only the seventh pitcher in Cub history to pitch a complete game shutout in his major league debut, and the first since Len "King" Cole in 1909. During the intervening decades, the closest effort had occurred on May 7, 1934, when Bill Lee went the distance to blank the Phillies, 2–0, in his first start. However, Lee had earlier made two relief appearances.

Signed by the Cubs in the 13th round of the June 1984 draft, Pico spent time in Pikeville, Peoria, Winston-Salem, Pittsfield, and Iowa before being called up to Chicago. Jeff's accomplishments in the bushes, while acceptable, were nothing to write home about by minor league standards. His best season was 1986, when he finished at 12–8 with a 3.20 ERA for Winston-Salem.

◆

Following his sensational entry into the majors, Pico had one more outstanding game in 1988. Filling in for the sidelined Mike Bielecki on August 27, Jeff held the Braves to four hits in a 5–0 distance performance. The bulk of his season was less effective. He finished at 6–7 with a 4.15 ERA.

Used sparingly in 1989, Pico was not a significant factor in the outcome of the season. He wound up with a 3–1 record with two saves and a 3.77 ERA. His final victory, in fact, was achieved with one pitch on September 30 at St. Louis.

The score was knotted up at 4–4 when Jeff entered with the bags loaded and one out in the bottom of the eighth. He induced Pedro Guerrero to ground into a double play on his first offering to snuff out the Cardinal rally. The Cubs then scored two in the ninth and held on to a 6–4 win as Les Lancaster held the Redbirds scoreless in their final at bat. However, the dramatics were anti-climactic since the Cubs had already clinched the division title four days prior.

As of this writing, Pico's future as a Cub appears to be uncertain. He is 9–8 in two seasons in the majors.

**B. Dec. 3, 1963, South Laguna, Calif.   BR,L TR   6'0"   205 lbs.**

# DAMON BERRYHILL

Courtesy of Chicago Cubs

Damon Berryhill's layoff cost the Cubs dearly in the playoff. The switchhitting catcher could have pulled the switch on the Giants with his solid bat and knowledge of Cub pitchers.

But Berryhill was placed on the disabled list following surgery on his sore right shoulder. That was the unkindest cut of all. It would've been nice to see him take his cuts at Candlestick.

Damon was originally selected by the White Sox in the 13th round of the January 1983 draft. He remained unsigned and continued his education at the little-known Orange Coast College in Costa Mesa, Calif. Berryhill gained all-conference honors as Orange Coast coasted to the championship.

The Cubs made Berryhill their first pick, and fourth overall, in the January 1984 draft. After three mediocre seasons at Quad City, Winston-Salem, and Pittsfield, Damon became a demon at Des Moines, blasting 18 homers in 1987.

♦

After Labor Day, 1987, Berryhill was called up to
the Cubs. He labored at bat, going 1-for-18, before
collecting four hits in his final 10 trips.

The 1988 season found Berryhill back in the
bushes. He was recalled from Iowa when Cub catcher
Jody Davis went on the disabled list.

Davis was popular with teen Cub fans, who
screeched "Jodee! Jodee! Jodee!" when the redheaded catcher would appear at the plate. But it soon
abated when they saw Berryhill throw out would-be
base-stealers.

After Davis returned, the Cubs were blessed with
two solid catchers. When Jody went into a June
swoon, Berryhill was there to fill in. He hit .395 with
15 hits in 38 trips, but strained his knee and went on
the disabled list. The job went back to Jody.

Berryhill hit his first big league grand slam
homer off Salome Barojas of the Philadelphia Phillies.
He began hogging the playing time against both
righty and lefty pitchers.

Cubs general manager Jim Frey became so en-
amored with Berryhill that he made his bold move by
trading Jody to the Atlanta Braves for a couple of
Kevins. They were pitchers Kevin Blankenship and
Kevin Coffman.

Berryhill wound up batting .259 with 7 homers
and 39 RBI and threw out 44 of 110 base-stealers. To
top his season, Berryhill was named catcher on Topp's
all-Rookie team. Also selected was first baseman
Mark Grace, making the Cubs the only team with two
rookies.

But nagging injuries continued to plague Berryhill. He opened the 1989 season on the disabled list.
That gave another rookie catcher a chance to catch
on. Joe Girardi opened the season behind the plate
and remained there until May 1.

That's when Berryhill came back with a big blast.
On his first day back from rehabilitation, Berryhill

♦

belted a 12th-inning homer to give the Cubs a 4–3 victory over the Giants. Damon then had a 4-for-4 day in an 8–2 triumph over the Reds. That helped the Cubs regain first place in May.

With Berryhill guiding the young pitchers, the Cubs remained in the pennant race. But Damon underwent arthroscopic surgery on his right shoulder on September 6 and was lost for the season. He finished with 5 homers, 41 RBI and a .257 average.

**B. Oct. 14, 1964, Peoria, Ill.   BR TR   5'11"   195 lbs.**

# JOE GIRARDI

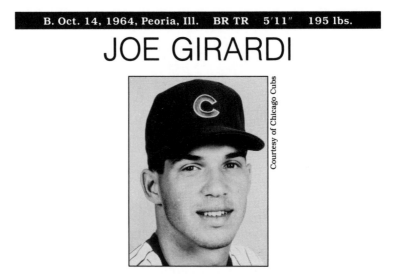

Courtesy of Chicago Cubs

The youthful Joe Girardi, basically a Cub back-up catcher in 1989, could conceivably play a major role in the future. It depends on how he develops, and how well Damon Berryhill comes back from his shoulder injury.

◆

A native of the same town as legendary Cub broadcaster Jack Brickhouse, Girardi is a graduate of Northwestern University, where he won All-American academic honors three times. The Cubs signed him in the fifth round of the June 1986 draft. With Winston-Salem of the Carolina League in 1987, he batted .280 and was selected for the All-Star team. The following season, promoted to Pittsfield of the Eastern League, he led the league in fielding average, putouts, assists, total chances, and caught stealing percentage. Again, he was an All-Star.

Were it not for a stroke of fate, Joe would not likely have been part of the 1989 Cub glory. Getting the job largely due to Berryhill's injury, Girardi was the Cubs' opening day catcher and remained their regular backstop until Berryhill recovered. While he displayed a strong arm, it was sometimes a wild arm. He fired seven balls into center field for throwing errors.

When Berryhill went out for the balance of the season, Rick Wrona was brought up from Iowa to share the catching chores with Girardi for the rest of the year.

Now under pressure, Girardi quickly learned to temper the wildness in his throwing arm. Instead of firing the ball over the second baseman's head, he nailed five straight runners trying to steal. He also proved himself adept at blocking runners charging into the plate. But his bat was disappointing as he hit only .248 in 59 games with one homer and 14 RBI.

For Girardi, a lifelong Cub fan who rooted for the ill-starred 1969 Cubs when he was not yet five years old, being on the parent team in the heat of a pennant race was both a dream come true and a maturing experience born of necessity. If his hitting comes around the way his fielding has, he could have a long career ahead of him.

◆

**B. Dec. 10, 1963, Tulsa, Okla.   BR TR   6'1"   185 lbs.**

# RICK WRONA

Courtesy of Chicago Cubs

Cubs fans squeezed into Wrigley Field on June 9 for a nationally televised night game against the despised New York Mets. It was a typical Cub-Met conflict.

The Cubs had a shaky 4–3 lead over the Mets in the ninth inning. As usual, Chicago partisans were waiting for the other shoe to drop. This time the villain was Kevin McReynolds, who homered off Cubs reliever Mitch Williams to tie the score, 4–4. The game remained tense well into the 10th inning.

In the bottom of the inning, Lloyd McClendon, who earlier homered for the third straight day, reached first on a Jeff McKnight error. Curt Wilkerson followed with a single and Shawon Dunston was hit by a Don Aase pitch to load the bases.

Cub manager Don Zimmer gave his Popeye squinch and looked down his bench. He had only one batter left. It was Rick Wrona, who had just arrived from Des Moines.

Zimmer put his arm around Wrona and whispered his instructions. Aah, strategy. Wrona nodded

♦

and strode to the plate. The capacity crowd was sensing some kind of bizarre play. Would Wrona swing away or bunt?

The left-handed batting Wrona squared off to bunt. The bat met the ball. Wrona laid down a beautiful suicide squeeze bunt that landed on the grass and died.

McClendon crossed the plate with the winning run and Wrona became the latest in a long line of heroes for the 1989 edition of the Cubs. But fame is easily forgotten. A few days later, Wrona was back in the bushes, a victim of numbers.

When Wrona was recalled from Iowa, the Cubs were squaring off with the Atlanta Braves August 25 at Wrigley Field. The team was mired in a six-game losing streak.

This time the teams were tied 3–3 in the 12th inning. Wrona got the Cubs off on the right foot with a solid single to lead off the inning. Domingo Ramos sacrificed Rick to second and Jerome Walton walked.

Ryne Sandberg singled to left and Wrona set off for home. He slid into the plate in a cloud of dust and the Cubs won 4–3. The kid catcher looked like a lucky charm.

The Cubs and Braves clashed again September 2 at Fulton County Stadium. There were no tense moments in this game. It was time to have some fun.

Wrona capped a six-run first inning with a three-run homer off Atlanta starter Marty Clary. It was Wrona's first big league homer and led the Cubs to a 10–3 laugher.

It was now late in the season. The September stretch drive was on and every game was bigger than life. The Cubs needed one victory to clinch the NL East title.

The Cubs were in Montreal for the crucial clash on September 26. Dunston reached base on an infield hit in the top of the second, bringing up Wrona.

Zimmer called for a hit-and-run and Rick responded by pulling Dennis Martinez's fastball down the left-field line for a triple as Dunston dashed home. The Cubs led 1–0 and went on to win 3–2.

It wasn't a Wrona-the-mill season for the non-rostered spring training catching fill-in. Although he wasn't a regular, the kid proved that he could perform when called upon.

**B. June 28, 1964, Winston-Salem, N.C.   BL TL   6'2"   190 lbs.**

# MARK GRACE

Courtesy of Chicago Cubs

If the Cubs continue as contenders in the 1990s, it will be largely because of the presence of young performers whose peak output should come during the upcoming decade. One such player who appears to be headed in that direction is first baseman Mark Grace, now entering his third year in the big time.

♦

Selected by the Cubs in the 24th round of the June 1985 draft, Grace broke into professional ball the following year with Peoria of the Midwest League. All he did was lead the league in batting with .342. In 1987, with Pittsfield of the Eastern League, he batted .333 and led the league in RBI with 101. That got him a 1988 promotion to the Cubs Triple A club.

As the 1988 season unfolded, the Cubs were rapidly losing confidence in their veteran first baseman, Leon Durham. With barely three weeks of Triple A experience behind him, Mark was summoned to the Cubs. Making his major league debut on May 2 at San Diego, he collected two hits. The following day, he hit his first big league homer off the Padres' Keith Comstock. The Cubs were so sold on him that they peddled Durham to Cincinnati two weeks later.

Playing 134 games, Grace knocked in 57 runs while batting .296, the highest average by a Cub rookie since Bill Madlock in 1974. On the minus side, his glove work at first base brought back memories of the Pirates' Dick Stuart years earlier—as his 17 errors attested to. In the voting for the Baseball Writers Association Rookie of the Year Award, Mark finished second to Chris Sabo of the Reds. Even so, he received a nice consolation prize in the form of *Sporting News* Rookie of the Year honors.

During the off-season, Mark labored day after day on his defensive play, emerging as a vastly improved first baseman in 1989. At the plate, he went from a good hitter to a better one. But his season could have come to an end because of an incident that happened on June 4.

Reportedly, there had been bad blood between Grace and pitcher Frank DiPino when the two were Cub teammates a year earlier. DiPino, now with the Cardinals, fired one that Mark interpreted as a brushback pitch, so he charged the mound, fists swinging. The bout was quickly broken up by umpires and

♦

teammates, with Grace suffering a minor shoulder injury in the process. Although the Cubs went on to an easy 11–3 victory, their first baseman was lost for three weeks on the disabled list. It could have been worse.

Fortunately, the mishap proved to be only a minor setback with no long term effects. Coming off his injury, Mark swung a hotter bat than ever, batting .347 with 34 hits, 10 doubles, 5 homers and 24 RBI for the month of July. These statistics won him the NL Player of the Month Award.

By the end of the season, the Cubs were number one in their division and Grace was the number one Cub hitter with a .314 average. He upped his homer count to 13 and his RBI total to 79, the latter figure being the team high. Moreover, he no longer looked like Dr. Strangeglove at first base, chopping his error count down to six. Because he struck out fairly seldom (42 times in 510 at bats), he was especially good when the hit and run was on. Mark attributed the bulk of his success to batting coach Joe Altobelli, saying, "He taught me how to think."

Cub fans were singing hymns to the praise of "Amazing" Grace. Equally pleased was Cub manager Don Zimmer, who remarked, "At the beginning of the season, people were asking me if he was going to have a what do they call it, sophomore slump. I said, 'No, this guy's just a hitter.'"

Finally, Frank DiPino said, "The thing between him and me is over as far as I'm concerned."

Grace added, "Me too."

During the Cubs' defeat in the league championship series, one of their few highlights was the hitting of Grace, who batted .647 with 11 RBI and 19 total bases. During the Cubs' lone victory over the Giants, a 9–5 triumph on October 5, Mark collected three hits. During the Cubs' six run inning in the bottom of the first, Grace contributed with a run-scoring double. In the sixth inning, his three-run double put the game on ice. The next day, *Chicago Tribune* sportswriter Jerome Holtzman called him "the new Billy Williams."

Whether or not Grace will turn out to be the next Billy Williams remains to be seen, but it certainly is a pleasant thought. For his first two major league seasons, Mark is a .305 hitter with 20 home runs and 136 RBI.

**B. Sept. 18, 1959, Spokane, Wash.   BR TR   6'1"   190 lbs.**

# RYNE SANDBERG

Courtesy of Chicago Cubs

It was Saturday, June 23, 1984, as the Cubs took on the Cardinals before a packed house at Wrigley Field. Cub fans all but slashed their wrists when the Cardinals took a 7–1 lead after two innings and a 9–3 margin after five and a half. But the Cubs clawed back like grizzly bears to chop the lead to 9–8.

♦

That was the score when Ryne Sandberg came to the plate with three hits already under his belt, leading off the bottom of the ninth. On the mound was Cardinal bullpen ace Bruce Sutter, who had previously held Sandberg to one big league hit in ten at bats. A couple of swings later, a split-fingered fastball sailed into the bleachers in left-center field. Sandberg had tied up the game. Cub fans yelled themselves hoarse.

When the game went into overtime, the cheers turned to groans as St. Louis rallied twice in the top of the tenth to make it 11–9. Two were out in the Cub half when Sutter walked Bobby Dernier in what appeared to be a case of prolonging the agony.

Suddenly, Sandberg was at the plate once again. Surely lightning could not strike twice at the same spot—but it did. Ryne homered again to knot up the game at 11–11, sending the crowd into a frenzy. One inning later, Dave Owen's single knocked in Bull Durham to give the Cubs a 12–11 victory in their most exciting comeback in many a year.

Although Owen had driven in the winning run, Ryne was the real hero with his five-for-six outing and seven RBI. "I'm in a state of shock," said Sandberg, who had gathered 24 hits in his last 48 at bats and 12 in his last 16. "I don't even know what day it is. I was going up there thinking about pulling the ball against Sutter. I wasn't even thinking about hitting one out."

Prior to the game, Cardinal manager Whitey Herzog said that Sandberg "may be the best player in the National League." After the contest, his words were, "Sandberg is the best player I have ever seen." It was the highlight of highlights in a dream season.

The Sandberg story began in Spokane's North Central High School, where Ryne excelled as a quarterback on the football team. He also played Little League and American Legion baseball.

Drafted by the Phillies in June 1978, Sandberg

♦

gained four years of minor league training at Helena, Spartanburg, Reading, and Oklahoma City. He was brought up to Philadelphia late in 1981 for his first major league trial, seeing action mainly as a late inning defensive replacement. Although he got into 13 games, he came to bat only six times, collecting one hit. On Jan. 27, 1982, Ryne and veteran shortstop Larry Bowa were traded to the Cubs for shortstop Ivan DeJesus.

Previously a shortstop, Sandberg was assigned the starting position at third base. He adjusted with grace and ease, making his defensive skills apparent from day one with his wide range and accurate throws.

With his bat, however, he stumbled off to one of the worst starts in recent memory, collecting only one hit in his first 32 trips to the plate. But manager Lee Elia refused to give up on him and more importantly, Sandberg believed in himself. Said Larry Bowa, "Ryne Sandberg never came close to panicking."

By the end of the season, Sandberg had jacked his batting average up to .271, collected 172 hits, and scored 103 times to lead the club. His 32 stolen bases set a high for a Cub third baseman, while he legged out 30 infield hits with his speed. In addition, he socked 30 doubles, five triples, and seven homers, driving home 54 runs.

Defensively, Ryne's .970 fielding average was exceeded only by the Cardinals' Ken Oberkfell with .972. In the National League Rookie of the Year balloting he finished sixth, but was given Chicago Rookie of the Year honors by the local writers.

Switched to second base in 1983, Sandberg made the transition with no difficulty, committing only 13 errors in 158 games to earn the Gold Glove Award. It was the first time in National League history that a player had won the Gold Glove his first year after being switched there from another position. His batting average slipped to .261, but he still led the club with 37 stolen bases and 94 runs scored.

The Cubs soon had a new manager, Jim Frey, who convinced Sandberg that he could improve his hitting by pulling the ball. As a result, the 1984 season became a time never to be forgotten, either for the Cubs or Sandberg.

Although Ryne started off slowly in the cold of early April, his bat soon turned into a red-hot iron. From April 24 through May 16 he hit safely in 18 consecutive games, batting .421 during the streak. He had 10 multi-hit games, including six straight three-hit contests. Sandberg ended up batting .373 for the merry month, gathering 41 hits. Since he generally batted second in the lineup behind former minor league teammate Bobby Dernier, the two became known as "the Daily Double."

Ryne began June in fine fashion, smacking two homers in a 12–3 racking of the Phillies that put the Cubs back in first place on the first of the month. In the weeks that followed his bat continued to blaze, reaching its zenith in the historic June 23 game.

By now Cub fans were calling Sandberg "the Natural" in reference to a hit movie starring Robert Redford as an amazing athlete who almost single-handedly led his team out of the briny deep into pennant contention—just as Sandberg was doing with the Cubs.

He had also become the heartthrob of screaming teenage girls, who swooned over him the way the bobby soxers of the early 1950s did over another Cub infield gladiator, Handsome Ransom Jackson. Ryne batted .373 for June, with 47 hits, 27 runs, eight homers, and 21 RBI, earning him the National League Player of the Month honors.

Meanwhile, "Ryno" had been running a distant third in the All-Star balloting for second baseman.

◆

Dodger Steve Sax, the front-runner, stated flatly that Sandberg deserved the honors, not he.

However, when the late returns came in, Sandberg was the people's choice, passing both Sax and Alan Wiggins of the Padres. At Candlestick Park on July 10 he played the entire game, collecting a single in four trips and stealing a base as the National League emerged victorious 2–1. It was the first Cub hit in an All-Star Game since Bill Madlock singled home two runs in the 1975 classic.

At the All-Star break Ryne was batting .335 with 118 hits, 11 homers and 52 RBI. Although his second half was less productive, Sandberg continued to deliver key hits and perform miracles at second base. When the Cubs clinched the National League East title at Pittsburgh on September 24, Ryne contributed a pair of doubles and scored the winning run on a single by Gary Matthews.

Finishing the season with a club-high .314 average, Ryno led the league with runs scored (114) and tied for the lead in triples (19), the most by a Cub player since Vic Saier had a club record 21 in 1913 (tied with Frank Schulte, 1911). He was second in the National League in hits with 200 and second in total bases with 331. His 36 doubles were good for a third place tie, while his .520 slugging average gave him sole possession of third.

Sandberg's 19 home runs were the most by a Cub second baseman since Rogers Hornsby's 39 in 1929, and his 84 RBI were the best at second since Billy Herman knocked home 93 in 1936. He came within one double and one home run of becoming the first player in major league history with 200 hits *and* 20 or more doubles, triples, homers, and stolen bases (he had 32 for the year) in the same season.

Defensively, Sandberg was better than ever. He made but six errors the entire season, best in the

♦

league, and played 61 consecutive games (June 29 through September 6) without a fumble, earning another Gold Glove.

In the pennant playoffs, Ryne missed a couple of tricky bouncers that went over his shoulder, but was otherwise a hero in a losing cause, batting .368 with seven hits, two RBI, and three stolen bases. Yet all the statistics combined cannot do justice to Ryne's contributions to the Cubs in their dynamic 1984 season.

It surprised no one when Sandberg coasted to the Most Valuable Player Award on November 13, the first Cub so heralded since Ernie Banks a quarter century earlier. "I was in my room taking a shower when the call came that I had won the award," he said. "I didn't even bother to dry off. I'm a little bit amazed. It's a great feeling, no question about it."

In 1985, Ryne almost duplicated his totals of the previous season, batting .305 with 26 homers and 83 RBI. Unchained on the basepaths, Sandberg stole 54 bases—the most by a Cub since Frank Chance pilfered 57 in 1906. Sadly, his teammates were unable to hang onto his coattails as the Cubs sagged to fourth place.

As the Cubs sputtered over the next three years, Sandberg's batting averages fluctuated between .264 and .294. He continued to excel on the field as the Gold Glove Awards began to pile up. This set the stage for an unforgettable 1989 season, both for the Cubs and for "Ryno."

In what was easily his best overall season in four years, Ryne batted .290 with 176 hits, a career high 30 home runs, 76 RBI, and 104 runs scored. At second base, he played a season record 90 consecutive games without a miscue, erasing the old mark set by former Cub Manny Trillo. To top if off, his 15 steals, although the lowest of his career, made him the first player since Johnny Evers to steal at least 250 bases

◆

**48**

in a Cub uniform. Moreover, on a team composed largely of young players, the veteran Sandberg served as a source of maturity and stabilization as the Cubs made their unexpected charge to the N.L. East title.

Sandberg had gotten off to a mediocre start, but quickly compensated for it in the second half of the season. From August 7 through 11, he smashed six home runs in five games to tie a Cub record set by Hack Wilson back in 1928. Obviously aided by Sandberg's hot bat, the Cubs won four of the five games; the only loss being a 16–13 slugfest with the Phillies on August 10. During the 24 games ending August 11, he had batted .353 (35 for 99) with 10 homers and 21 RBI. Interestingly, all 10 round trippers had come during the last 15 games. "I don't consider myself a player who can do that," Sandberg remarked of the impressive power surge. "It just happens." From July 28 to the end of the season, he was .346 with 18 homers and 38 RBI.

Unfortunately, the Cubs ran out of magic in the league championship series, as the Giants crushed them in five games. Although Sandberg, like some of the others, continued to hit well, Cub pitchers were overwhelmed by Giant home run bats. At the close of the playoffs, Sandberg said, "There's nothing to be ashamed of. We weren't supposed to be here, and we did better than anyone expected. We're young and we're going to stay good." Hopefully, history will prove him to be correct.

Through 1989, Sandberg is a .285 lifetime hitter with 139 homers and 549 RBI. At age 30, he should have some fine years yet ahead of him.

♦

**B. Oct. 1, 1956, Boise, Idaho    BR TR    6'2"    185 lbs.**

# VANCE LAW

Courtesy of Chicago Cubs

Vance Law is the son of Vern Law. His mother's name is VaNita. His brothers are Velton, Veryl, Vaughn and Varlin. His sister is VaNita. Vance had a pet dog named Victor, who was reportedly run over by a Volkswagen—or was it a Volvo? With the Cubs, Vance helped pile up victories.

Vernon Law was a pitching standout with the Pittsburgh Pirates, compiling 162 victories and 147 losses from 1950 to 1967. His best season was 1960 when he had a 20–9 record, plus a 2–0 mark in the World Series, and won the Cy Young Award.

The bespectacled Vance Law is Vern Law's only offspring to spring into the major leagues. Vance made his big league debut with the Pirates in 1980, but batted only .230 in 25 games as a spare infielder. After hitting .134 the following season, the Pirates made him walk the plank.

He was traded to the Chicago White Sox with pitcher Ed Camacho on Mar. 21, 1982, for pitchers Ross Baumgarten and Butch Edge. The Sox gained the edge in that deal after Law emerged as a regular infielder, batting .282 that season.

Law saw action at second base, shortstop, and third base when the Sox won the 1983 American League West Division title, with "Winning Ugly" as their rallying cry.

The Sox scene turned Sox ugly in the 1983 playoffs against the Baltimore Orioles, and Law played a minor role. One of those "what if" situations hounded the Sox.

The Orioles were leading the best-of-five series 2–1. The fourth game was scoreless in the seventh inning when Greg Walker and Law opened with singles. The play called for a bunt to move the runners along.

On a 3-and-1 count, Jerry Dybzinski did bunt, but Orioles catcher Rick Dempsey pounced on the ball and forced pinch-runner Mike Squires at third. Julio Cruz followed with a single to left, but Dybzinski rounded second base too far and got caught in a rundown.

Vance Law, attempting to score, was gunned down at the plate. Three hits and a bunt and no runs. The Orioles scored in the 10th inning for a 3–0 victory, sending Baltimore to the World Series and the Sox reeling. That loss probably softened Law for future heartbreak with the Cubs.

After hitting only nine homers in two Sox seasons, Law muscled up with 17 homers in 1984. But the Sox were desperate for relievers and dispatched Law to the Montreal Expos for pitcher Bob James on Dec. 7, 1984.

Law was a semi-regular for three seasons at Montreal. He filed for free agency and was signed by the Cubs Dec. 12, 1987. The Cubs, not noted for going out for flesh in the free agent market, needed anything that could move at third base.

The deal was one of general manager Jim Frey's best moves. After watching Ron Cey and Keith Moreland stand almost stationary at third base, Law's mobility was most welcome.

♦

Vance batted a personal high .293 with the Cubs in 1988. His 78 RBI were within one of team leader Andre Dawson, whose two-run homer in the final game enabled him to regain the lead.

Law even gained a berth on the All-Star team. He played the ninth inning at second base, his only action at that bag all season. Vern and Vance thus became the third father-son All-Star combo in history, following the Boones (Ray and Bob) and the Bells (Gus and Buddy).

Although the Cubs rose to the top of the NL East in 1989, Law was no big noise from Boise. Vance was in and out of the lineup with nagging injuries and wound up sharing the bag with newly acquired Luis Salazar. In the off season before the 1990 season, Vance decided to take his talents overseas to tackle the Japanese version of the American pastime.

**B. May 19, 1956, Barcelona, Venez.  BR TR  6'0"  185 lbs.**

# LUIS SALAZAR

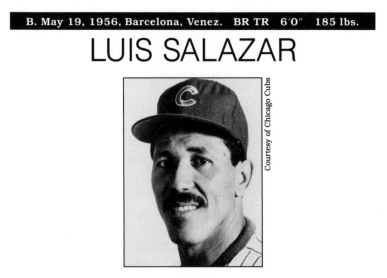

Courtesy of Chicago Cubs

Seldom has a late-season acquisition paid such early dividends with the Cubs. Luis Salazar, a well-travelled

♦

journeyman infielder-outfielder, was acquired from the San Diego Padres August 31 with Marvell Wynne for Darrin Jackson, Calvin Schiraldi and Phil Stephenson.

And it was just in time. In his first 17 games with the Cubs, Salazar batted .392, with 20 hits in 51 trips, including five doubles, a homer, 11 RBI and three game-winners.

Luis produced perhaps the two biggest hits of the season. Gloom and impending doom settled in the Cubs clubhouse after they blew a rain-delayed 7–2 lead over the St. Louis Cardinals September 8 at Wrigley Field.

After more than an hour wait, the game was resumed in the seventh inning. The Cards rallied for four in the seventh and five in the eighth, went on to win 11–8 and cut the Cubs' division lead to a half-game.

The following day was dank, dark, damp and drizzly. And the Cards were leading 2–1 with two outs in the eighth inning. A St. Louis victory would tumble the Cubs out of first place. That's when Luis rode to the rescue.

Salazar singled home Dwight Smith with the tying run at rainy Wrigley. The contest went into the 10th inning. With one out and gimpy-kneed Andre Dawson on first, Salazar doubled into the right-field corner.

Dawson cut the corners on his creaky joints, limped around third and splashed home in the mud for a 3–2 triumph. The win restored the Cubs' lead to 1½ games, prompting manager Don Zimmer to call it "our biggest win of the year."

That clutch contest probably disposed of the Cards. But there was still the New York Mets, who came to town the following week. Newly acquired lefty Frank Viola and the Mets were leading 3–2 in the fifth inning. Salazar pumped one into the seats with a man aboard in the bottom of the fifth for a 3–2 lead. The pumped-up Cubs went on to romp 10–6.

♦

Salazar finished the season, hitting .325 in 26 games and could be more than a stop-gap third baseman even at age 34. Despite his potent bat, the native of Barcelona, Venezuela has banged around the bushes and the big leagues.

His career in organized ball began at Sarasota in 1974. From there he bounced around Niagara Falls, Salem, Buffalo, Portland, and Hawaii. Salazar served three terms with the Padres and short stretches with the White Sox and Tigers in between. He's hoping for a long stretch with the Cubs.

**B. March 21, 1963, Brooklyn, N.Y.   BR TR   6'1"   175 lbs.**

# SHAWON DUNSTON

Courtesy of Chicago Cubs

After four years of inconsistent promise, shortstop Shawon Dunston appears to have matured as a ballplayer. Thanks to a brilliant second half, he was a prime factor in helping the Cubs to a division championship. Hopefully, his previously enigmatic play is a thing of the past.

A baseball star at Thomas Jefferson High School in Brooklyn, Dunston was selected by the Cubs in the first round of the June 1982 draft. This made him the highest draft pick in New York City history.

After signing with the Cubs, Dunston was dispatched to Sarasota, where he tied for the lead in stolen bases with 32, while batting .321. Promoted to the Quad Cities in 1983, he raised his base stealing count to 58 and batted .310.

In 1984, Dunston advanced to Midland and was hitting .329 when he was transferred to Iowa. Shawon found Triple A pitching considerably more formidable, batting only .233.

Nevertheless, with the aging Larry Bowa nearing the end of his career, the Cubs were in desperate need of a new shortstop, whether Dunston was ready for the majors or not. On opening day of 1985, Shawon was the Cubs' starting shortstop. He collected his first major league hit on April 9, a single off Pittsburgh's Rick Rhoden, and his first big league home run off San Diego's Greg Booker on May 4. However, he obviously needed more seasoning, so on May 15 he was optioned to Iowa after batting just .194 and committing nine errors. Recalled on August 13, Dunston batted .320 from August 23 to the end of the season, collecting 47 hits in 137 at bats. Lifting his overall batting average up to .260, he now appeared ready for big league competition.

By 1986, Bowa had hung up his spikes and Shawon had the shortstop's job all to himself. Although Dunston batted only .250 for the year, his 17 homers and 68 RBI were the most by a Cub shortstop since Ernie Banks (29 and 80) back in 1961. He hit .276 with men in scoring position, and his 36 doubles were third in the league. His 14-game hitting streak was the longest of the season by a Cub player.

♦

Defensively, he was frequently spectacular but just as often erratic. He led the league in putouts (320), assists (465), and total chances (817), and was tied for the league lead in double plays (96). Unfortunately, his 32 errors were high in the NL also. Although Shawon covered plenty of ground and made many a breath-taking stop, his throwing errors brought back memories of Roy Smalley, a wild-throwing Cub shortstop of the late 1940s and early 1950s.

If 1986 was Dunston's first memorable season, then the next year was a season to forget. Sidelined from June 16 to August 21 with a fractured ring finger on his right hand, he played only 95 games in 1987, batting .246. All five of his home runs came before the injury, and he drove in only 22 runs.

By early 1988, Shawon appeared to have finally put it all together. He was batting .287 with 42 RBI by the All-Star break. He had also seemingly attained consistency with his glove. Dunston felt honored when he was named to the All-Star team, even though he did not play. Then, in an unexplainable nosedive, he hit only .202 with 14 RBI for the rest of the season, as his average for the year skidded to .249. Once again, the sweetness had turned sour. Even so, his 257 putouts were tops in the NL, while he was the Cubs' best base-stealer with 30.

When the off-season began, so did the trade rumors. As early as November, unverified whisperings of the press had him going to the Pirates, the Expos, and the Mets at one time or another. "Do they have to trade me?" Dunston queried in an interview. "I don't want to go anywhere. I want to play my whole career in Chicago."

The rumors turned out to be nothing more than that, as Shawon was still a Cub when the 1989 season opened. But his batting slump continued and reached its nadir, as he struggled to bat even .200 during the early months of the season. His grandmother, to whom he had been very close, died of cancer on April 23, and this doubtlessly affected him emotionally. When he was hampered by a hamstring injury, Domingo Ramos filled in at shortstop and performed well.

Despite Ramos' hot bat, manager Don Zimmer refused to give up on Dunston. As soon as Shawon was well, he was back in the lineup. By All-Star time, his batting average was back up to .238, but he continued to lack consistency at the plate. Zimmer stuck with him, saying, "he is my shortstop and I want him to know that."

It was around that time that the Shawon-O-Meter made its appearance. A group of fans in the left field bleachers at Wrigley Field had taken a special liking to Shawon. They made a sign which followed his batting average. Whenever Dunston had an official time at bat, the numbers were adjusted accordingly.

Evidently inspired by his manager's and fans' confidence, Shawon began relaxing at the plate and stopped swinging at pitches that were two feet outside—one of his most glaring weaknesses. From the All-Star break onward, his numbers rose steadily, as well as his spirits. Defensively, he learned how to control his powerful arm. The combination of Dunston and Ryne Sandberg gave the suddenly resurrected Cubs the most feared double play combo in the NL.

In the weeks that followed, Dunston went on a batting rampage that made the Shawon-O-Meter rise 40 points. He earned NL Player of the Week honors for the week of September 11–17. He went 11 for 21 with his first career grand slam and eight RBI. The Shawon-O-Meter was going berserk.

By the end of the year, Shawon had raised his batting average to .278, with nine homers and 60 RBI. Only Mark Grace, Andre Dawson and Ryne Sandberg

♦

drove in more runs among Cub players. Trade talk had become ancient history. Said Dunston, "I was here when they were losing and I was dedicated to the team. I was proud to be a Cub even when we were in last place. I don't want to leave while we are winning and having all this fun. I'm still a dedicated Cub and always want to be a Cub."

If late 1989 was a sign of things to come, then Cub fans will always want him to remain at Wrigley Field also. Through last season, Shawon is a .256 lifetime hitter with 569 hits, 44 homers, and 224 RBI.

B. July 10, 1954, Miami, Fla.   BR TR   6'3"   195 lbs.

# ANDRE DAWSON

Courtesy of Chicago Cubs

In three seasons with the Cubs, Andre Dawson went from awesome to almost awful, but the team climbed from last to first. And don't bury Dawson at wounded knee.

♦

After spending ten solid seasons with the Montreal Expos, Andre Nolan Dawson was tired of playing on artificial turf and went searching for splendor on the grass. He played out his option and became a free agent in 1987.

The grass he sought was in Chicago. But Dallas Green and the Cubs were sweeping out their high-salaried help. In addition, they seldom sought free agents.

Dawson practically went to his wobbly knees to wear a Wrigley Field uniform. He agreed to sign for a bargain basement salary, an estimated $500,000. And what a bargain he became.

Andre was the first bonafide long-ball threat on the Cubs since they had Dave Kingman. Dawson even topped Kingman's top Cub homer total, 49 to 48, and drove in a whopping 137 runs, the most by a Cub right fielder. His 49 homers ranks him second to Hack Wilson's 56 in 1930 among all Cubs.

Despite Dawson, the Cubs finished last in the National League West. Without Dawson, the Cubs would have finished in Dubuque. In addition to his power hitting, he continued to wear a Gold Glove in right field. Andre earned his seventh Gold Glove as an outfielder. In one game Dawson's strong arm was an eye-popper. He threw out Roger Mason at first base on an apparent single.

At the conclusion of the 1987 season, the man they call the "Hawk" was named the NL's Most Valuable Player, was selected Player of the Year by the *Sporting News*, the Associated Press and *Baseball America*.

Dawson deserved the awards because he was downright destructive. He hit a club record 15 homers in August—three shy of the major league record held by Rudy York of the Detroit Tigers in 1937.

Twice he hit five homers in three games. He hit three homers in one game and hit for the cycle in

♦

another. In addition, Dawson had 16 game-winning hits.

But his hottest streak came against the Houston Astros, June 1–2, at Wrigley Field, when he drove in 12 runs. Dawson found the confines very friendly at Wrigley Field, averaging a homer every 10.8 at-bats.

Perhaps his proudest moment came in his final at-bat of the season at Wrigley Field. His new-found fans were clamoring for a homer—and he obliged. When he raced out to his position he was greeted by "salaams."

To sum up the season, Dawson was awesome to opponents, was held in awe by his teammates and was adulated by Cub fans. Dawson enjoyed the limelight. After playing in virtual obscurity in hockey-mad Montreal, Dawson was in demand for endorsements and commercials.

And when he returned home, the city of South Miami renamed a street Andre Dawson Drive. It must be a street of line drives.

What could the Hawk do for an encore in 1988? First, he signed for megabucks, joining teammate Rick Sutcliffe on millionaires row.

Although his power production dwindled to 24 homers and 79 RBI, he again led the Cubs. Dawson did raise his batting average from .287 to .303 and garnered his eighth Gold Glove as a ball Hawk. He even stole home and again homered in his final Wrigley Field at-bat.

Dawson started slowly in 1989, went on the disabled list, returned to the lineup and went on a hot streak. Then he faced more surgery, but came back strong to help the Cubs clinch the NL East title.

After having his knee drained in April, Andre went into May with only two homers. Moreover, his batting average dropped to .236 and his strikeouts mounted. But he wobbled to the plate in May and went on a tear, collecting 10 hits in 11 at-bats.

♦

Included in his barrage were three triples and three homers, raising his average to .307. On May 7, in Los Angeles, he homered twice and singled twice against the Dodgers for a 4–2 Cub victory. The following day he beat out an infield hit, stole second and rose slowly.

He flexed his right knee repeatedly, batted twice more in the game, and again submitted to arthroscopic surgery. Andre then joined center fielder Jerome Walton and left fielder Mitch Webster on the disabled list. The entire outfield was wiped out.

Somehow, the Cubs hung tough with their hero-a-day routine. Upon his return, Dawson joined in the fun on August 15 by blasting a three-run homer in the 12th inning to rout the Reds.

Being in and out of the lineup proved costly. Dawson yielded his RBI leadership to first baseman Mark Grace, 79 to 77, and lost out to second baseman Ryne Sandberg in homers by a wide margin, 30 to 21.

But Dawson served as an elder statesman on a team populated with youngsters like Shawon Dunston, Jerome Walton, and Dwight Smith, who looked to his leadership down the stretch to the NL East title.

In the playoffs against the Giants, the Cubs' field of dreams was nightmarish for Dawson as Don Zimmer's Boys of Autumn took a pratfall—dropping four of five games. Playing on threadbare knees, Dawson left 17 runners on base in the abbreviated series.

He wound up with a bundle of strikeouts and a .105 batting average. Although this was the bleakest moment of his brilliant career, he never let loose with any tantrums. In reality, the fault wasn't placed entirely on Andre's broad shoulders. Zimmer's pitching staff fizzled out, especially against a chap named Will Clark.

Back in 1975, Dawson wasn't taken by the Expos until the 11th round of the June draft because of his knee problems, which began at South Miami Senior High School where he played football.

♦

He spent only two seasons in the bushes, hitting 41 homers with a .612 slugging average. Andre batted .330 at Lethbridge in 1975 and divided the season between Quebec (.357) and Denver (.350) before being called up to the big leagues. His first hit came off Phillies' ace Steve Carlton on September 13.

In 1977 Dawson was selected NL Rookie of the Year after setting an Expos rookie record of 19 homers. He hit his first major league homer off Atlanta's Buzz Capra on May 18.

Dawson was now in the center field spotlight with Montreal. He was flanked by left fielder Ellis Valentine and right fielder Warren Cromartie. The trio was billed as the outfield of the future. Only Dawson prevailed.

Andre saved his biggest moments for Wrigley Field. He clouted his 200th homer off Cub pitcher Steve Trout on Sept. 23, 1985. The following afternoon Dawson drove home eight runs with a first-inning homer and a pair of three-run homers in the fifth inning. The six RBI in one inning tied a major league record.

People wondered how Dawson would do playing 81 games at the Friendly Confines. Andre covered himself with ivy-covered glory by belting 49 homers. But that's all in the past. What's ahead for the 35-year-old graybeard with the woeful knees? Hopefully, the Hall of Fame in Cooperstown, New York.

**B. Aug. 8, 1965, Newnan, Ga.   BR TR   6'1"   175 lbs.**

# JEROME WALTON

Courtesy of Chicago Cubs

Going into the 1989 season, it had been 27 years since a Cub player had won the coveted Baseball Writers Association Rookie of the Year Award. John Kennedy was in the White House and Krushchev was in Moscow when it had last happened. The memory of Ken Hubbs in 1962 had become a faded image to those who recalled him, while many a younger Cub fan had the impression that only other teams were destined to have the best rookies. That all came to an end with the arrival of Jerome Walton.

Selected by the Cubs in the second round of the 1986 draft, Jerome looked like a coming star with Class A Peoria of the Midwest League in 1987. With Double A Pittsfield of the Eastern League in 1988, he lead the circuit with a .331 average. Nevertheless, he had yet to compete even in Triple A ball, much less the majors.

By spring training of 1989, the Cubs were down to one outfielder with a guaranteed spot in the lineup,

◆

right fielder Andre Dawson. Don Zimmer told Walton he would open the season with him if he could hit .260 in the spring.

Instead, Walton swung at a .280 clip, leading the team in hits with 23. When the Cubs broke camp, Walton was the starting center fielder and leadoff man, a spot he would never relinquish.

On April 4, 1989, Jerome made his major league debut a dubious one, dropping Mike Schmidt's flyball in the second inning before 33,000 at Wrigley Field. Cub fans wondered what this kid was doing in the majors, but their favorites came back to edge the Phillies, 5–4.

The puzzlement turned to cheers when Walton displayed a major league bat. But when he pulled a hamstring on May 10, during a game against the Giants, Jerome found himself on the disabled list until June 11. The following day, he celebrated his return by collecting four hits in a 10–3 romp over the Mets. On June 17, he singled in the winning run to give the Cubs and Rick Sutcliffe a 3–2 victory over the Expos. This was a big win, because it snapped a three-game losing skid and began a five-game winning streak.

By now, Jerome had a road roommate in the person of Dwight Smith, himself a rookie who had never been beyond Double A ball. They became close friends, giving each other encouragement as the campaign went on. "It helps a lot because we can talk on the same level," Walton said in mid-season. "We can communicate as rookies and it makes it a lot easier."

As the Cubs began to gather steam after the All-Star break, so did Walton's bat. By August 11, he had hit safely in 22 straight games as the Cubs clipped the Phillies, 9–2. On August 19, his hitting streak reached 29 games to exceed the 20th century Cub high of 28 set by Ron Santo in 1966. He reached 30 the following day. However, the Cubs, in the middle

♦

of a six-game losing streak, lost both games to Houston by 8–4 scores. On August 21, Walton's hitting streak came to a halt at 30.

During that time, Walton was 46 for 136, good for a .338 average. The Cubs had gone from third place, 3½ games out, to first place, 2½ games ahead. By now, both Walton and his team were in the national spotlight. His streak was four games short of the rookie record set by Benito Santiago of the Padres in 1987.

Although there were no more spectacular hitting streaks, Jerome continued to play solid ball. He finished the season with a .293 average, 139 hits, 6 homers, and 46 RBI. His 24 stolen bases were high for the club, while his batting average was seventh highest in the league among those who qualified for the title.

Thanks to his hitting streak, Walton was a cinch for Rookie of the Year honors. It came as no surprise when he received 22 of 24 first place votes during the balloting on November 8. Roommate Smith, who received second in the voting, got the other two. "I'm glad he's runner-up," said Jerome. "I'm glad I won. I know Dwight will be happy for me, just like my other teammates are. He told me we could make the ballclub out of spring training and try to finish 1–2. We really just were trying to pump each other up all season."

As for being the Cubs first Rookie of the Year in more than two and a half decades, he said, "I don't know about 1962. I'm happy right here in 1989." Hopefully, he will remain happy and productive as a Cub for years to come.

**B. Jan. 1, 1959, Gary, Ind.   BR TR   5'11"   195 lbs.**

# LLOYD McCLENDON

Courtesy of Chicago Cubs

Lloyd McClendon joined the Cubs in the nick of time with a timely knock. The entire Cub opening-day outfield was on the disabled list when McClendon was recalled from Iowa on May 15, 1989.

Right fielder Andre Dawson was out with a knee injury, center fielder Jerome Walton was sidelined with a pulled hamstring, and left fielder Mitch Webster was nursing a thigh injury.

The Cub bats were virtually silent. They produced a total of five earned runs in as many consecutive losses. Moreover, the team fell to fourth place in the NL East—3½ games out of first. They were about to drop out of sight.

McClendon, a pudgy product from Gary, Indiana, was inserted into left field. He hit a three-run homer in his first at-bat. The Cubs went on to whip the Atlanta Braves 4–0 behind Mike Bielecki and Calvin Schiraldi. That pivotal game sent the Cubs soaring. They won four in a row and were back in the race.

◆

In addition to left field, Lloyd was employed at first base, filled in at third base, and even went behind the plate as an emergency catcher. The 30-year-old journeyman could also hit.

As a youngster, Lloyd Glenn McClendon participated in the 1971 Little League World Series in Williamsport, Pennsylvania. He was 5 for 5 with 5 homers and 5 walks. But Taiwan beat Gary in the championship game.

McClendon was originally selected by the New York Mets in the eighth round of the June 1980 draft. But it was a long road to the majors, beginning with Kingsport in 1980. McClendon first made headlines Dec. 16, 1982, when the Mets dealt him and pitcher Tom Seaver to the Cincinnati Reds.

While Seaver reported to Cincy, McClendon saw service in Little Falls, Lynchburg, Waterbury, Vermont, Wichita, Denver, and Nashville. He showed punch by pounding 24 homers at Denver in 1986. The homer total led all players in the Cincinnati farm system.

McClendon finally emerged from the bushes for short stints in the big leagues in 1987 and 1988. But his .208 and .219 batting averages weren't impressive. Perhaps the Cubs were impressed when McClendon hit a two-run pinch homer off Greg Maddux on June 1, 1988, at Wrigley Field.

To make room for McClendon, the Cubs traded outfielder Rolando Roomes to the Reds on Dec. 9, 1988. McClendon was on the spring roster, but saw little action and was dispatched to Des Moines.

He came back with a bang and displayed much-needed versatility. He replaced Mark Grace at first base when Mark suffered a shoulder separation and was on the disabled list from June 5 to June 23.

McClendon eased the loss of Grace by homering in three straight games in a crucial series against the Mets. While Grace was gone, McClendon hit safely in 9 of 11 games, with 4 homers and 10 RBI.

♦

When Grace returned, manager Don Zimmer platooned McClendon with rookie Dwight Smith in left field. Lloyd wound up with 12 homers, 40 RBI, and a solid .290 average.

If the Cubs ever win a pennant with McClendon, Lloyd will be the fifth player to participate in the Little League and big league World Series. The others are Boog Powell, Jim Barbieri, Rick Wise, and Carney Lansford.

B. Nov. 8, 1963, Tallahassee, Fla.   BL TR   5'11"   175 lbs.

# DWIGHT SMITH

Courtesy of Chicago Cubs

Dwight Smith was a mess in Mesa, was demoted to Des Moines, came back to the Cubs, and made a run for rookie honors—all in one season.

When the Cubs traded Rafael Palmeiro to the Rangers, their long-range plans last spring included

Smitty in left field. Smith, however, didn't live up to the Cubs' expectations and was sent back to Iowa.

After injuries decimated the entire Cub outfield, Smith was recalled. He responded by hitting .324, the highest Cub average by a rookie since Hack Miller clubbed .352 in 1922.

Smith is best known as the hero of the biggest comeback victory in Cub annals. He drove in the tying and winning runs in their 10–9 thriller over the Houston Astros August 29 at Wrigley Field. After Astros shortstop Raul Ramirez hit a grand slam homer, Houston assumed a 9–0 lead. Going into the bottom of the sixth inning all seemed lost. Manager Don Zimmer took out slugger Andre Dawson and replaced him in right with Smith.

The Cubs tallied two in the sixth and three in the seventh, with Smith singling home a run. Our hero then bounced back with a clutch game-tying sacrifice fly in the eighth inning as the Cubs rallied for four more runs.

It was 9–9 going into the tenth inning. Rookie Jerome Walton opened with a walk and was sacrificed to second by Ryne Sandberg. Lloyd McClendon singled Walton to third. McClendon took second on that throw, bringing the hot-hitting Mark Grace to the plate.

The Astros walked Grace intentionally to load the bases for Smith. It was Astros ace reliever Dave Smith against Dwight Smith. Dwight outdid Dave by slapping a single to right field. As Walton waltzed home with the winning run, Smitty was mobbed by his teammates.

But it wasn't all that easy for Smitty. He was recalled May 31 and made his major league debut by going 0-3 against the Giants at Candlestick Park. Perhaps his miserable spring training was no fluke.

It wasn't until June 5 that Smith became an integral part of the Cubs surge. He hit his first big

♦
**69**

league homer, a three-run shot off David Cone, as the Cubs mauled the New York Mets 15–3 at Wrigley Field.

Smitty showed his versatility by singing the national anthem before the July 21 game against the Giants at Wrigley Field. It was the first time a Cub performed the anthem since third baseman Carmen Fanzone played the trumpet June 18, 1972.

Smith then put a close game out of reach with a pinch–grand slam homer in the sixth inning for a 10–2 Cub triumph over the Phillies, July 31, at Veterans Stadium.

In a nationally televised game against the Mets (July 28), Dwight again proved he wasn't just another Smith. The Cubs were trailing 5–2. In the seventh inning they rallied for four runs behind Smith's two-run blast into Wrigley's right field bleachers. The Cubs won 6–5.

It wasn't all right with Dwight. He later poked a homer to left against St. Louis and a strong wind. Smith's homer helped turn a 1–0 Cardinals lead into a 4–1 Cub win on September 10.

Smith's potent bat helped the Cubs clinch the NL East title with a 3–2 victory September 26 in Montreal. His sixth inning single drove in Ryne Sandberg to give the Cubs a 2–0 lead. In the eighth inning, Smith singled to right field, and when Hubie Brooks bobbled the ball, Sandberg scored all the way from first base with the winning run.

Smith wound up the season with nine homers and 52 RBI in addition to his .324 average. But it couldn't offset teammate Jerome Walton's slick center fielding and 30-game hitting streak, which thrust him into the national spotlight.

Dwight celebrated his 26th birthday by finishing second to Walton as NL Rookie of the Year. Smith, the only player named on all 24 ballots, had two first place votes, 19 second and one third for a 68 total.

♦

Smith was selected by the Cubs in the third round of the June secondary draft in 1984. In five minor league seasons he stole 207 bases. The future looks bright for Dwight.

**B. April 26, 1961, Petersburg, Va.   BR,L TL   5'9"   173 lbs.**

# CURT WILKERSON

Courtesy of Chicago Cubs

Although considered a throw-in for the trade that sent Rafael Palmeiro to Texas for Mitch Williams, infielder Curt Wilkerson added some pinch-punch for the 1989 Cubs. In addition to filling in at second base, short-stop, and third base, Wilkerson had a .360 average as a pinch-hitter.

The stocky switch-hitter had nine pinch-hits in 25 at-bats and raced around the bases with many game-winning runs. Remember when pitcher Les Lancaster doubled in the 11th inning to give the Cubs a 4–3 come-from-behind victory over the Giants July

♦

20 at Wrigley Field? It was Wilkerson who chugged around the bases and slid home with the winning run in the nationally televised game. And guess whose two-run single tied the score with two out in the ninth? Again it was Wilkerson.

Curt always seemed to click when the Cubs performed before a nationwide audience. On June 8, when second baseman Ryne Sandberg was hurting, Wilkerson stepped in and collected four hits.

It was Wilkerson's hit that sent Lloyd McClendon to third base, where he scored on Rick Wrona's suicide squeeze bunt.

And on September 23 against the Pirates, he reached base safely on a Jose Lind error to lead off the ninth inning. Domingo Ramos bunted him to second and he raced home on Mitch Webster's pinch-single for a 3–2 Cub win.

Wilkerson was selected by the Texas Rangers in the fourth round of the June 1980 draft. At that time he was strictly a right-handed batter. The Rangers converted him to a switch-hitter to enhance his value as a speedster.

During his tenure in Texas, Wilkerson seldom played a regular role. He began as a shortstop, but soon filled in at all infield positions. Perhaps his biggest day was against the White Sox at Comiskey Park on June 2, 1988. Curt was 4 for 5 with three runs scored, three doubles and three RBI, including the game-winning blow.

Cub manager Don Zimmer is counting on Curt to be a versatile utility infielder for quite a few more seasons.

# Passing Ships:
# Future Talent,
# Rusty Veterans

**B. July 5, 1951, Colorado Springs, Colo.   BR TR   6'3"   225 lbs.**

## GOOSE GOSSAGE

Courtesy of AU Sports

With his Fu Manchu mustache, Clint Eastwood slit
eyes and barrel chest, Richard Michael Gossage was
an imposing figure on the mound. Success followed
Gossage from the bush leagues to the big leagues—

◆

until he reached the Cubs. By then the Goose was cooked.

Gossage, one of few players to come out of Colorado, signed with the Chicago White Sox after being selected in the ninth round of the June 1970 draft.

The big right-hander was the Big Apple at Appleton in 1971. He led the corps with an 18–2 record, 1.83 ERA, 7 shutouts, and 15 complete games. In addition, he struck out 149 batters in only 187 innings.

The following season found Gossage in a White Sox uniform, where he posted a 7–1 record. The White Sox converted Gossage to a reliever with good results. The Goose hooked up with portly Terry Forster and a nifty right-left relief duo was formed.

The pair remained intact after they were sent to the Pittsburgh Pirates for slugger Richie Zisk and pitcher Silvio Martinez in December 1976. With the Pirates, Gossage set a relief record of 151 strikeouts in a career-high 72 games.

That fall he was granted free agency and signed for a big salary with George Steinbrenner of the New York Yankees. Gossage supplanted Sparky Lyle as ace of the Yankee bullpen. He led the league in saves with 27 and was named Fireman of the Year in 1978.

Perhaps his biggest moment came that same season when he induced Red Sox slugger Carl Yastrzemski to pop out in the ninth inning to clinch the American League playoff win over Boston.

From then on, Gossage was the Yankees' savior, frequently getting the call in tight situations. He appeared in six straight All-Star games.

Gossage soon tired of Steinbrenner and escaped the Bronx zoo by opting for free agency. The Goose was gobbled by the San Padres in 1984. It was the Goose who stopped the Cubs that autumn in the National League playoffs, closing out victories in game 3 and game 5.

♦

Gossage soon moved into second place in career saves behind Rollie Fingers, 341 to 289. And he was among the leaders in all relief categories.

The Goose remained the big guy in the Padres pen the next three years, despite losing a little zip off his fastball. He was now ripe for the Cubs, who surrendered outfielder Keith Moreland for his relief services on Feb. 12, 1988.

Gossage's one season as a Cub was gut-wrenching. Some of his relief appearances sent Cub fans home ready to kick their dogs. He registered a 4–4 record with only 13 saves. Sometimes he was only one out or one strike away from victory. Although sometimes it wasn't entirely his fault, he let games slip away.

Wrigley Field patrons rarely razz any player in Cub flannels. But after a grand slam homer on August 11 by the Mets' Kevin McReynolds with two out and two strikes that turned a 4–2 Cub lead into a 6–4 loss, the Goose was a lame duck.

Somehow, Gossage remained the whole season. But he drew his release during spring training in 1989. Gossage was soon picked up by the San Francisco Giants as manager Roger Craig's reclamation project. After failing to protect leads, he was released by the Giants. He soon found refuge again in Yankee pinstripes.

♦

**B. Nov. 11, 1962, Sellersville, Pa.    BL TL    6'0"    170 lbs.**

# JAMIE MOYER

Courtesy of Chicago Cubs

Jamie Moyer enjoyed a few moments of Cubs glory during his short term in a Chicago uniform. His 12 strikeouts against the Philadelphia Phillies on April 13, 1987, were the most by a left-handed pitcher in a nine inning game.

Moyer also had another fantastic adventure. He fanned seven straight Giants for a club record on July 3 at Wrigley Field. But Jamie was the victim of poor support by his mates.

For instance, his 12–15 mark in 1987 was deceiving. The Cubs were shut out three times and scored only one run in three other contests that season. Overall, the Cubs tallied only 23 runs in his 15 defeats.

Success came early for the southpaw, whose mound posture resembled Groucho Marx before he delivered the ball. As a high schooler in Souderton, Pennsylvania, he tossed three consecutive no-hitters.

After games, Moyer and his mates would stop at a fast-food hamburger joint and watch the proprietor

♦

flip the burgers. The flipper was Bobby Shantz, a lefty who compiled a 119–99 record, including a 24–7 season with the old Philadelphia Athletics in 1952.

Although Moyer drew many scouts, he preferred the books to batters and attended St. Joseph's University in Philadelphia. Because his fastball wasn't overpowering, Moyer wasn't selected by the Cubs until the sixth round of the June 1984 draft.

The Cubs sent the slim lefty to Geneva, but he was too fast for that competition. In a half-season, Moyer was 9–3 with 120 strikeouts in only 109 innings. Moyer started off with an 8–2 mark at Winston-Salem in 1985 and quickly emerged with the Cubs in 1986.

Jamie joined the Cubs on June 14 and finished with a 7–4 record. Included was a two-hitter on August 16 as he blanked the Expos 5–0 in Montreal. At that time it appeared Moyer had a brighter future than both Greg Maddux and Les Lancaster, among other hurlers.

However, in 1988, the same year Moyer married the daughter of Notre Dame basketball coach Digger Phelps, batters were beginning to hit his pitching. After posting a disappointing 9–15 record, Jamie was no longer a Cub untouchable.

The Cubs included Moyer as part of the Rafael Palmeiro package in a nine-player deal with the Texas Rangers on Dec. 6, 1988. The trade was blasted by Cub partisans. It didn't help when Moyer got off to a 3–0 start with the Rangers.

But Moyer developed arm trouble and spent most of the season on the disabled list. He wound up with a 4–9 mark and his earned run average ballooned to 4.86. After four big league seasons Moyer has a 32–43 record, 28–34 with the Cubs.

**B. Nov. 12, 1956, Gainesville, Ga.   BR TR   6'4"   192 lbs.**

# JODY DAVIS

Courtesy of Chicago Cubs

"Jo-dee! Jo-dee! Jo-dee!" The crescendo reached its peak in the sixth inning as 32,403 fans, jammed into Wrigley Field, shouted for a carrot-topped catcher to kiss one out of the park.

Ron Cey was walked intentionally to load the bases on Sept. 14, 1984, when Jody Davis selected a warclub and strode to the plate to face Mets' pitcher Brent Gaff.

"I heard the people screaming and I got the chills," said Davis. "It really got the adrenalin going. But when you're up there with the bases loaded, you try to put the crowd out of your mind and concentrate on what you're doing."

Gaff let loose with a fastball and Davis drove the first pitch into the left-center field bleachers for a grand slam homer. That blow helped lift the Cubs and Rick Sutcliffe to a 7–1 victory and put them eight and one-half games ahead of the Mets in the National League East race.

As he churned the bases, the fans chanted, "Jo-dee! Jo-dee! Jo-dee!" They didn't stop until Davis returned to the dugout, came out, and doffed his cap. Late heroics were getting to be a habit with the popular Davis.

Perhaps his most dramatic homer of the season occurred on May 12 against Houston at the Astrodome, which is hardly a homer haven. The Cubs were trailing 4–2 with two out and two on in the top of the ninth.

Jody appeared as a pinch hitter against reliever Frank DiPino. He hit a 3–0 pitch over the center field fence for a 5–4 Cub triumph. Only this time he was greeted by deafening silence.

The strong-armed young catcher was originally drafted by the Mets in 1976 after starring in high school and American Legion ball. In one legion game, Jody hit three homers, one a grand slam, and drove in eight runs. He was twice voted Most Valuable Player at Gainesville's North Hall High School, where he also lettered in basketball.

Davis reported to Marion of the Appalachian League in 1976, but batted only .232. It wasn't until 1979 that Davis blossomed into a hitter, batting .296 with 21 homers and 91 RBI at Jackson of the Texas League. His batting instructor at that time was Phil Cavarretta, the old Cub favorite.

The Mets, however, were touting John Stearns as their backstop of the future and Davis was sent to the Cardinals organization for pitcher Ray Searage. He was purchased for $25,000 by the Cubs on Dec. 8, 1980.

Jody never saw a big league ballpark until he arrived at Wrigley Field at the outset of the 1981 season. He spent much of the early part in the bullpen as third stringer behind Tim Blackwell and Barry Foote.

The Cubs were sleep-walking at the start of the season and Blackwell and Foote did their bit. Foote went 0-for-22 and was shipped to the Yankees. The walrus-mustached Blackwell fared a little better, but Davis remained a spectator.

It wasn't until June 5 that manager Joey Amalfit-ano realized the Cubs had nothing to lose by giving

♦

Davis a good shot. Jody got three hits in a victory over the Dodgers and the Cubs won four of five with Davis behind the plate.

It took a midseason strike to stop Jody. When play resumed in August, Davis was the Cubs' No. 1 catcher. He was a take-charge guy, ordering the pitchers to throw more inside pitches. "You can't survive in this league by pitching outside and down the middle," insisted the rifle-armed receiver.

Davis finished with a .256 average, 4 homers, and 21 RBI. During the winter he was named Chicago Rookie of the Year by the local writers.

But he was just another face when the Cubs assembled for spring training in 1982. The team had a new general manager, Dallas Green, a new manager, Lee Elia, and a new catcher, Keith Moreland, all from the Phillies.

With those odds the job was automatically handed to Moreland, who started off with a hot bat and a cold glove. Baserunners were taking liberties with Moreland. Despite his .382 average Keith was hurting the team on defense.

Elia finally moved Moreland to the outfield and reluctantly handed the job back to Jody, who celebrated with a game-breaking homer against the Astros on May 9 at Wrigley Field.

The score was tied 3–3 in the bottom of the ninth. The Cubs had two runners aboard with two out and a full count on Davis. Reliever Randy Moffitt fired a fastball and Jody "hit the hell out of it," said Elia. The ball sailed onto Waveland Avenue for a 6–3 victory.

The Cubs seemed more complete with Davis behind the plate. Although he wound up with a .261 average and chased pitches that were a bit low and outside, Davis displayed some extra base power with 20 doubles and a dozen homers to go with 52 RBI.

Davis progressed as a batter in 1983. He stopped trying to pull outside pitches and learned to stroke

♦

the ball to right field. But his 23 passed balls were disturbing.

It wasn't disturbing, though, to hear "Jo-dee! Jo-dee! Jo-dee!" That was popularized during a three-game series against the Cardinals that drew 116,107 fans to Wrigley Field in mid-June. That's when Davis stroked three homers and drove in 10 runs. Among his blows was his first grand slam in the fourth inning off Bob Forsch on June 12.

Jody's 24 homers tied Ron Cey for the team lead. In addition, he had 31 doubles and 84 RBI and upped his average to .271. His homer total was the most by a Cub catcher since the heyday of Gabby Hartnett.

Davis cut his passed ball total to nine in 1984 and set a personal high of 94 RBI, the most by a Cub catcher since Gabby (who else?) drove in 122 in 1930. In addition, Davis collected 19 homers.

Best of all, Davis provided a memorable moment for Cub fans when pitcher Rick Sutcliffe blew a third strike past Pittsburgh's Joe Orsulak in the ninth inning on September 24 at Three Rivers Stadium.

Davis held the ball aloft and clutched Sutcliffe. Baseball's redheaded battery had led the Cub charge to the National League East Division title.

While many of the 1984 Division heroes slowed to a walk, Davis remained a Cub mainstay. The kid from Gainesville continued his iron-man role behind the plate, playing 415 games the next three seasons.

After slugging 17, 21, and 19 homers, Davis trailed only Gabby Hartnett in career power production by a Cub catcher. He shared the Cub homer title with Gary Matthews in 1986 with 21 each.

Davis also tied Hartnett with 5 grand slam homers each. Only Ernie Banks (12), Bill Nicholson (8) and Billy Williams (8) slammed more. Jody was the Cubs starting catcher in six straight openers from 1983 through 1988.

Nagging injuries and the emergence of youngster

♦

Damon Berryhill cut into Jody's playing time in 1988. Moreover, Davis slid into disfavor with Cub management by belly flopping along the infield tarp with five others during a rain delay in the Cubs first Wrigley Field night game on Aug. 8, 1988.

Following that incident Davis pounded the pines, pining away. He wished he was back in Dixie.

Davis was granted his wish of marching back to Georgia. He was dealt to the Atlanta Braves for a pair of unknown Kevins—Blankenship and Coffman. Davis thus finished his Cub career with 122 homers, 11th on their all-time list.

Jody's departure ended an era for the Cubs. He was the last to play under the Wrigley regime.

Perhaps it was just in time for the Cubs because Jody fell from first to second to third string catcher with the Braves in 1989. His final figures were a sickly 4 homers, 19 RBI and a .169 batting average.

**B. July 31, 1957, Cincinnati, Ohio   BL TL   6'2"   210 lbs.**

# LEON DURHAM

Courtesy of Chicago Cubs

♦

At one time, Leon "Bull" Durham seemed destined to be a key to future Cub hopes. In the long run, these hopes were left unfulfilled.

In high school Leon played baseball, basketball, and football, earning letters in all three. In his senior year, he batted .385 and was 11–3 on the pitcher's rubber. This caught the attention of the ever-vigilant St. Louis Cardinals' scouting staff, who signed him in the June 1976 free agent draft. He was dispatched to the Cardinals' rookie team in Sarasota, Florida, where he remained the rest of the season.

During the next two years, Durham polished his skills at Gastonia, St. Petersburg, and Arkansas. By 1979 he was ready for the Cardinals' Triple A team in Springfield, Illinois, of the American Association. He came through with a .310 average, 23 homers, and 88 RBI to earn Rookie of the Year honors.

The Bull started the 1980 season with Springfield, but was soon called up to the Cardinals. There he batted .271 in 96 games, singling off Met pitcher Mark Bomback in his major league debut.

Meanwhile, the Cubs had a problem on their hands in the person of Bruce Sutter, the bullpen ace. After an arbitrator had ruled in Sutter's favor during contract negotiations the previous spring, the Wrigley organization did not want to hold his $700,000 contract, so up he went on the trading block.

General Manager Bob Kennedy had his eyes on Durham, and went to St. Louis hoping to use Sutter as his ace in the hole. But Card front office boss Whitey Herzog, playing on Kennedy's twin anxieties to unload Sutter and grab Durham, apparently maneuvered him into taking Ken Reitz, an over-the-hill third baseman, and Tye Waller, a second-stringer—along with Leon—in exchange for Sutter. So instead of returning to Chicago with a full house, Kennedy went home with what looked like a handful of deuces.

Reitz lasted one year in a Cub jersey while Waller

◆

remained a bench-warmer. Durham, however, paid dividends. In the 1981 season, hampered by a player's strike, Durham batted .290 in 87 games, led the club in stolen bases with 25, triples with 6, and tied Bill Buckner for the home run lead with 10.

The following year Leon began charging after pitches like a bull in a china shop, finishing with a solid .312 average in his first complete season, tops on the Cubs and third in the league. Moreover, he paced the team with 7 triples and 22 home runs while his 33 doubles, 90 RBI, and 9 game-winning hits were second to Buckner. Durham's fielding continued to improve, and he did not suffer a prolonged slump all year.

Following Bull's splendid display in 1982, there were great expectations. Unfortunately, Bull saw action in only 100 games in 1983. His batting average dropped to .258 as he was bothered with hamstring and shoulder problems all year. Most of his 12 homers and 55 RBI came early in the season. A healthy Bull could have made the difference in many a Cub loss.

In the spring of 1984 it was decided to move Leon to where he would be least likely to get injured—first base. When Durham took over at that position, Wrigley Field fans received him with a resounding chorus of boos. They chanted "We want Buckner," for the star who had been the fixture at first for seven years. The jeers turned into cheers, however, when Bull led the Cub charge through the early months of the season. And Buckner was soon a memory, being traded to Boston for pitcher Dennis Eckersley.

The Bull gored National League hurlers in May, ripping them for a .351 average, nine homers, and 34 RBI, earning him Player of the Month honors. On May 8 he became the first Cub player, since Dave Kingman in 1979, to homer in four straight games. He drove in four runs as the Cubs outslugged the Giants 10–7 at Wrigley Field.

But the most dramatic act came at St. Louis on

♦

June 10. It was the top of the ninth as the Cubs nursed a 1–0 lead with the bases loaded. Leon was at third with Jody Davis at second and Larry Bowa at first. Suddenly, while the Cardinals were bird napping, Bull broke for the plate—and made it! With all eyes on Durham, Davis stole third and Bowa took second. It was the Cubs' first triple steal in so long that nobody could (and still cannot) remember when it last happened.

The Cubs held on to win 2–0. After the game, Cardinal manager Whitey Herzog said, "The Cubs are the best team I've seen."

Just as Leon appeared to be approaching super stardom, his old nemesis came back to haunt him at Wrigley Field on June 24. He jammed his right shoulder while diving back to first base to avoid a pickoff. The following day he was placed on the 15-day disabled list.

At the time of his mishap, Durham was batting .308 with 12 homers and 52 RBI. When he returned to the lineup after the All-Star break, his second half was somewhat of a letdown as his average tailed off to .279. Even so, Bull's 23 homers and 96 RBI marked career highs and were second on the Cubs to Ron Cey.

In the pennant playoffs against the Padres, Durham emerged as both a hero and a goat. In the second game, October 3, he played a sparkling defense to help preserve a 4–2 Cub victory at Wrigley Field, giving Chicago a 2–0 series lead. At San Diego, October 6, he powered a game-tying home run in a contest that the Cubs went on to lose 7–5, to tie up the series at two apiece.

Then came the tragic finale on the following day. The game began promisingly enough when Leon's two-run homer gave the Cubs a 2–0 lead in the first inning. Another by Jody Davis made it 3–0 in the second.

By the bottom of the seventh, the Cub lead had been whittled to 3–2. With one out and Carmelo Martinez at second, Tim Flannery's grounder went

♦

through Durham's legs like water through a sieve, enabling Martinez to score, tying the game. San Diego rallied to take a 6–3 lead and shut out the Cubs the rest of the way, winning the game and dashing Chicago's pennant hopes. "The ball stayed down. It didn't come up," said Durham at the Cubs' wake. "I make that play 200 times in a row." Ironically, it was only his eighth error of the year.

Following the 1984 season, Leon's accomplishments were largely disappointing. Although he continued to put forth an acceptable output, batting .282 in 1985, .262 in 1986, and .273 in 1987, Durham failed to reach the superstar potential he showed during his early years. More ominously, he stopped stealing bases and hitting with runners on base, as his RBI total declined every year.

In 1987, Bull's last full season with the Cubs, the Wrigley Field wrecking crew went on the biggest home run binge in Cub history, sending 209 baseballs into orbit. Between April 24 and 28, Leon almost looked like the Durham of old, smashing four homers in as many days. It was essentially his last hurrah as a Cub. Although he hit a career high 27 homers for the season, he drove home only 63 runs, a meager total for a regular first baseman or anyone else with that many home runs.

By 1988, the Cubs were grooming Mark Grace to be their new first baseman. Durham no longer fit into their rebuilding plans. On May 18, he was traded to the Reds for pitcher Pat Perry. Although Leon seemed pleased at the chance to play before his hometown fans, he spent most of the time on the bench and was suspended because of an alleged substance abuse problem.

Released by the Reds in October of 1988, Bull signed on with his original team, the Cardinals. In St. Louis, he saw practically no action. By the end of 1989, he was again on the suspended list.

Through 1989, Leon is a .278 lifetime batter with

♦

147 home runs and 530 RBI. With his baseball career presently in jeopardy, one can only speculate where he will be in 1990.

**B. Dec. 25, 1950, Edo Monagas, Venez.   BR TR   6'1"   150 lbs.**

# MANNY TRILLO

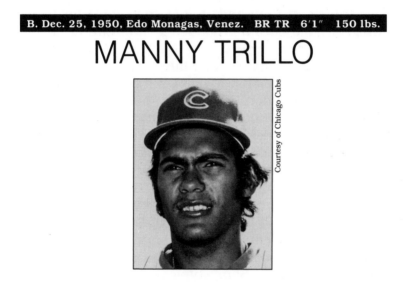

Courtesy of Chicago Cubs

Wolves were howling at the Cubs' door when they acquired Manny Trillo. And many were howling in laughter when they dealt him away. The slim native of Venezuela was never fully appreciated in a Cub uniform.

Trillo, tall, dark, with a boyish, sly grin, gave the Cubs four seasons of artistic play at second base, something they lacked before his arrival and after his departure.

There must be something in the Venezuelan air or water that grows such smooth, fluid infielders as Chico Carrasquel, Luis Aparicio, Dave Concepcion, and Manny Trillo.

◆

Signed originally by the Philadelphia Phillies in 1968, Trillo's minor league credentials were as slim as he is trim. "Trillo can't hit. . . . He has no strength," read some of the scouting reports. He was written off as a big league prospect.

Manny proved them wrong. After hitting .302 at Des Moines in 1972 and .312 at Tucson the following season, Trillo became the center of attention during the 1973 World Series.

A's owner Charles O. Finley tried to get rid of second baseman Mike Andrews, because of several clutch errors. When Finley tried to replace him with minor leaguer Trillo, Andrews' teammates revolted. Andrews was quickly reinstated to his position and Trillo was shipped back to the bushes.

His name didn't crop up again until Oct. 23, 1974, when he was sent to the Cubs in a three-for-one deal. He was accompanied to Chicago by relievers Darold Knowles and Bob Locker. In return the A's received long-time Cub hero Billy Williams.

The consensus of opinion was that the Cubs were victims of a heist. Some typical comments: "Worst Cub trade since the Lou Brock for Ernie Broglio deal," and "How stupid can the Cubs be, giving up a player of Williams' caliber for three guys nobody knows."

The lone dissenter was Cubs' general manager John Holland, the victim of the Brock debacle. "Trillo is the key man," said Holland. "We needed a second baseman and we think we got one who can field with anyone."

Holland was right. After second baseman Glenn Beckert ran out of gas in 1973, the Cubs' keystone brigade of 1974 resembled the Keystone Kops with such comics as Vic Harris, Rob Sperring, Billy Grabarkewitz, Ron Dunn, and Matt Alexander on the beat.

Trillo took charge in 1975 and stopped all that traffic. Having veteran Don Kessinger as a double-play

◆

partner helped. "He's one of the easiest guys I've worked with," said Kessinger. "He doesn't have a good arm. He has a great arm."

Cincinnati Reds' manager Sparky Anderson proclaimed Trillo's arm "the best I've ever seen. Bill Mazeroski had a quicker arm, but not as strong," said Sparky.

Cub broadcaster Lou Boudreau, a Hall of Fame shortstop, also praised Trillo. "Joe Gordon's the best I've ever seen," said Boudreau. "Manny's right up there with Joe."

There was a bit of hot dog in Trillo's repertoire that irked batters going down the line to first base. Manny would scoop up the ball, hesitate until the runner got close to the base, and then whip the ball with a quick sidearm motion. It agitated the runners, but Cub fans ate up his act.

Manny's hitting proved a bonus. Although he batted .248, Trillo proved tough in the clutch, driving in 70 runs. It was the most by a Cub second baseman since Don Johnson drove in 71 in 1944.

Trillo's average dipped to .239 and he had 59 RBI in 1975, but he tightened the defense with 527 assists and took part in 111 double plays.

In 1976 Trillo teamed well with shortstop Ivan DeJesus as the "Latin Connection." They were a busy double-play combo with both topping the league in assists. Trillo had 467 and DeJesus 595.

Then followed what was supposed to be Trillo's big year. He led the league in hitting at .362 in mid-June. His main hitting rival was outfielder Dave Parker of the Pittsburgh Pirates.

The 6'5", 250-pound Parker came to Wrigley Field and crossed bats with the 150-pound Trillo in a photo. Parker looked like he could devour Trillo for breakfast.

While Parker continued to eat up National League pitching and eventually win the batting title at .338,

♦

Trillo slipped badly and finished with a .280 mark. Manny was a prime example of a player wilting in day games under the hot sun at Wrigley Field. In addition, Trillo played all winter in Venezuela. It took its toll on the slight athlete.

Despite his nosedive at the plate, Trillo continued to make spectacular plays afield. The DeJesus-Trillo tandem was now the best in the league. In 1978 they teamed for 1,036 assists, tops in the majors.

Meanwhile, the Philadelphia Phillies were climbing in the standings. They lacked only a second baseman to put them over the top. They eyed Trillo. They dangled three benchwarmers and the Cubs' GM Bob Kennedy fell into the trap.

After haggling all winter the trade was consummated on Feb. 23, 1979. The Cubs received second baseman Ted Sizemore, outfielder Jerry Martin, and catcher Barry Foote, plus minor league pitchers Derek Botelho and Henry Mack for the coveted Trillo. The Cubs even threw in outfielder Greg Gross and catcher Dave Rader.

Surprisingly, the Chicago media and Cub fans hailed the trade, citing Trillo's midseason fadeouts at the plate. Martin, Foote, and Sizemore became instant Cub regulars.

But the Cubs sank from the pennant chase and the three were dispersed in trades. Trillo, meanwhile, thrived on the Astro-Turf carpet at Veterans Stadium.

He was the hero of the storied 1980 championship playoff against the Houston Astros, batting a rousing .381, and he earned a World Series ring as the Phillies downed the Kansas City Royals in six games.

The Gold Glove Awards he deserved as a Cub also came his way. The Phillies knew when to get on the Gold standard. Trillo was acknowledged as the best fielding second baseman in 1979, 1980, 1981, and 1982.

He then became a much-traveled Trillo, bouncing

♦

from the Cleveland Indians to the Montreal Expos to the San Francisco Giants, spending much of his time on the disabled list.

Following two largely unproductive seasons in San Francisco, Manny found himself traded back to the Cubs on Dec. 11, 1985, for infielder Dave Owen. Although only used on a part-time basis, the aging Trillo provided some spark to a lackluster Cub roster. He was given a warm return welcome by his many fans in Chicago.

In 1986, despite missing more than a month with a fractured right thumb, Trillo got into 81 games by filling in at first, second, and third base. He batted .296. With men in scoring position, he batted .341 and drove home 18 runners. Coming in as an early inning replacement on August 13, he collected three hits, including a home run as the Cubs outslugged the Pirates, 9–8.

Manny continued to be an outstanding utility man the following season. He appeared primarily at first and third, but occasionally played second and short, also. It was a season that included both heroics and personal milestones.

On June 7, 1987, his two-run homer off Doug Sisk of the Mets, with two out in the bottom of the ninth, gave the Cubs an exhilirating 4–2 victory. Career hit number 1,500 came in Atlanta on August 19 during a 9–1 Cub win. For the season, he was .294 in 108 games, with a personal high eight home runs. As a pinch-hitter, he garnered seven hits, including his first pinch home run on July 29. It was one of the few highlights of an 11–3 drubbing at the hands of the Expos.

Manny was used more sparingly in 1988, as his batting average fell to .250. Declaring free agency during the off-season, he signed with the Reds. In Cincinnati, he came to bat only 39 times, collecting eight hits. Through 1989, Trillo is a lifetime .263 hitter with 1,562 hits, 61 homers, and 571 RBI.

♦

**B. Sept. 24, 1964, Havana, Cuba    BL TL    6'0"    180 lbs.**

# RAFAEL PALMEIRO

Courtesy of Chicago Cubs

The town in which Mississippi State University is located was more like Sparkville than Starkville in 1984. Sparking the Bulldogs was a baseball troika of Will Clark, Bobby Thigpen, and Rafael Palmeiro.

The trio batted 3–4–5 in the lineup. Clark became a Giant clouter, Thigpen the main man in the White Sox bullpen, and Palmeiro joined the crosstown Cubs.

Rafael Corrales Palmeiro swatted .415 with 29 homers and 94 RBI that season to become the first Triple Crown winner in Southeastern Conference history. His homer and RBI totals were second and third in the nation.

The Cubs boasted a hot property when they drafted Palmeiro in the first round of the June 1984 draft. He was the 22nd player chosen. The Cuban-born Palmeiro was originally selected by the New York Mets in the eighth round of the June 1982 draft, but elected to get a college education.

After taking center stage in Starkville, the Cubs wanted to see how Palmeiro played Peoria. Rafael got

♦

into 73 games, and drove home 51 while collecting 22 doubles and hitting .297.

Then it was on to Pittsfield of the Eastern League in 1986, where he won Most Valuable Player honors with his league-leading 156 hits and 95 RBI, plus a .306 average.

The Cubs thought Palmeiro was worth a late-season trial. He made his big league debut September 8 and he got his first hit and RBI off Tom Hume of the Phillies. The following day, Palmeiro connected for a three-run homer off the Phillies Kevin Gross.

Even more impressive was Palmeiro's ability to get his bat on the ball. He had only six strikeouts in 73 at-bats. It appeared a star was born. But after spring training Palmeiro wound up on the cutting room floor.

The Cubs were loaded with left fielders and decided to platoon Jerry Mumphrey and Brian Dayett. Rafael went from left field to left out in the cornfields of Iowa, which was no field of dreams.

Palmeiro was recalled on June 16 and he made the most of it, especially the dog days of August and September. He hit safely in eight of nine games in August and from September 18 on he batted .381 with 5 doubles and 5 homers. Rafael concluded with 14 homers in a half-season.

Moreover, he became a fan favorite, a sort of Latin Lothario with bright brown eyes and a ready smile. And Palmeiro didn't disappoint in 1988. For most of the season he chased San Diego's Tony Gwynn for the batting title, finishing second with a .307 average.

They don't trade .300 hitters—or do they? On Dec. 6, 1988, Rafael became a Ranger. Cubs general manager Jim Frey was bombarded with hate mail.

He was the big name in a complicated nine-player deal. In addition to Palmeiro, the Texas Rangers received pitchers Jamie Moyer and Drew Hall. Traded to the Cubs were pitchers Paul Kilgus, Steve Wilson, and Mitch Williams, plus infielder Curt Wilkerson. And two

◆

days later the deal was completed with the Cubs receiving minor leaguers Luis Benitez and Pablo Delgado.

It appeared to be a one-sided deal. Palmeiro, teamed with Ruben Sierra and Julio Franco as "The Three Amigos," rode roughshod through the American League. Franco finished with a .316 average and Sierra batted .306, but Palmeiro plummeted to .275 on a late-season slump.

Frey was taken off the frying pan when Mitch Williams emerged as the Cubs "Wild Thing" in the bullpen and newcomer Dwight Smith batted .324 as Palmeiro's replacement in left field.

B. Sept. 26, 1964, New York, N.Y.     BL TL     5'10"     150 lbs.

# DAVEY MARTINEZ

Courtesy of AU Sports

For a brief period, Davey Martinez appeared to have the Cub center field job nailed down. Instead, he ended up being swapped in a one-for-one deal just as he was becoming a familiar fixture.

♦

Signed by the Cubs in the January 1983 draft, Martinez split that season between their farm clubs in the Quad Cities and Geneva. The following season, he spent nearly the entire campaign on the disabled list with injuries to his left knee and hamstring. But when he batted a league-leading .342 for the Cubs' Double A club in Winston-Salem in 1985, the brass began to take notice.

Promoted to Triple A Iowa in early 1986, Davey was rushed up to Chicago on June 14 in hopes that he would be ready to face major league pitching. Unfortunately, he was not. Following an 8-for-67 streak, Davey was sent back down, finishing his Iowa season at .289. Recalled on September 2, he was used seldom during the remainder of the year, batting only .139 as a Cub.

By 1987, however, Davey looked like he had a fine future as a Cub. Switched to the leadoff spot in mid-June, he raised his batting average from .256 to .292 by the end of the season. His eight triples were high on the Cubs and eighth in the NL. He also displayed fair speed, pilfering 16 bases.

On the minus side, Davey hit only eight home runs while driving in a meager 36 runs—poor totals for a man stationed in center field, normally a power position. His 96 strikeouts did not help either.

It was Martinez's lack of home run prowess that prompted the Cubs to trade him to the Expos for outfielder Mitch Webster on Bastille Day, 1988. Although Davey and his teammates were shocked by the trade, the Cub management was hoping that Webster, who had hit 15 homers the year before, would help prop up their sagging clout.

As it turned out, the trade was neither a gain nor a loss for the Cubs. While Webster was a major disappointment in Chicago, Martinez's career has likewise been on the downswing. Following his fine 1987 season, he batted .255 the following year and

♦

.274 last season. Entering the 1990 season, he is a .263 lifetime batter with 362 hits, 18 homers, and 126 RBI.

**B. Sept. 9, 1952, Tyler, Tex.    BR TR    6′2″    200 lbs.**

# JERRY MUMPHREY

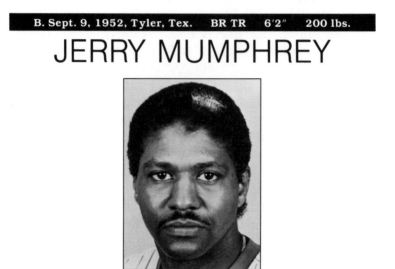

Jerry Mumphrey was a competent but generally un-noticed ballplayer who never quite made it to genuine stardom during his 15 years in the major leagues. Yet for two seasons—1986 and 1987—he was the heart of the Cub bench and one of their finest pinch-hitters in recent memory.

By the time Mumphrey came to the Cubs, he was already a veteran. During his previous twelve seasons, Jerry had roamed the outfield for the Cardinals, Padres, Yankees, and Astros. His one season at San Diego in 1980 was perhaps his best overall. He batted .298 with 168 hits and 52 stolen bases in 160 games.

♦

He batted .300 in 123 games for the Yankees in 1982. At Houston, two years later, he drove in 83 runs for a career high. Although his batting averages were generally good, Jerry was not a power hitter, and had limited defensive skills. This consigned him to the role of a baseball wanderer.

On Dec. 16, 1985, Houston traded Jerry to the Cubs for outfielder Billy Hatcher and pitcher Steve Engel. Spending the following season as the Cubs' top utility flychaser, Jerry got into 111 contests, batting .304 with 32 RBI. As a pinch-hitter, he was 10-for-29 (.345) with a homer, two game-winning hits, and 8 RBI. Three of his five home runs came against the hated New York Mets, including a game-winning, three run, pinch-hit homer off Roger McDowell on August 5 to give the Cubs and Lee Smith an 8–5 victory.

In 1987, Jerry was again the full-time part-timer par excellence. He lifted his batting average to .333 in 118 games with 13 homers (six against the Phillies) and 44 RBI. As in the previous season, his batting average was the best on the Cubs, but he did not have enough times at bat (only 309) to qualify for the official club leadership. Off the bench, Mumphrey was 12 for 35 with 12 RBI and a .343 average, second highest among NL pinch-hitters.

Among the dozen pinch-hits were a pair of round-trippers, a two run job off Steve Bedrosian of the Phillies on April 12 and a three run homer off Kent Tekulve, also of Philadelphia, on June 18. The Cubs split these contests, losing 9–8 in 10 innings in April but holding on 9–7 two months later.

Following these performances Jerry had high hopes for being promoted to a full-time position in 1988. But by that time, the Cubs had assembled a regular outfield in Andre Dawson, Rafael Palmeiro, and Davey Martinez; the latter being replaced by Mitch Webster in mid-season. There were also allega-

♦

tions that Jerry and new manager Don Zimmer did not see eye to eye concerning Mumphrey's role on the team. Consequently, he came to bat only 66 times, batting .136.

By now, it was clear that Mumphrey no longer fit into Cub plans, probably due to advancing age and slowness afield. Released after the 1988 season, he finished his career a .289 hitter with 1,442 hits, 70 homers, and 575 RBI.

# 1987
# Gene Michael Takes Charge (Sort of)

B. Aug. 4, 1934, Newport, Del.   BL TR   6'5½"   210 lbs.

## DALLAS GREEN

Jimmy Piersall hammered a hanging curve for his 100th career homer and ran the bases backwards. Pete Rose found the ideal pitch to unload the lone grand slammer of his career. In both instances, the pitcher was Dallas Green.

♦

The rangy right-hander became a 20-game winner, but it took him eight years. Toiling for the Phillies, Senators, and Mets during the 1960s, Green compiled a 20–22 lifetime record. Thus, adversity was nothing new for the wavy-haired *wunderkind*.

Dallas Green is a winner. Like a surprising number of other baseball executives whose playing careers were less than spectacular, Green proved to be outstanding as a manager and in the front office. His Phillie minions were staked to their lone World Series title feast under Green's thumb in 1980. And before he managed, Green served as the Phillies' farm director, producing a bumper crop.

When the Cubs moved from the Wrigley Building to the Tribune Tower, Green came on to rid the team of its losing image. "I'm not here to win friends," drawled Dallas. "I'm here to win ball games."

Like John Wayne, he showed true grit by turning goners into gamers. When he finished mopping up, only three players (Leon Durham, Lee Smith and Jody Davis) remained.

"Every trade we made, we were criticized," said Green. "Especially during the early days." Cub fans howled when shortstop Ivan DeJesus was swapped for shortstop Larry Bowa. But a throw-in was a kid named Ryne Sandberg.

Add Rick Sutcliffe, Steve Trout, Bob Dernier, Gary Matthews, Keith Moreland, Ron Cey, Dennis Eckersley, Scott Sanderson, and a steady hired-hand named Jim Frey and you have a National League East champ. From last to first in three seasons!

It was Green who put all the pieces of the puzzle in place. But Dallas wanted the big prize—a World Series winner at Wrigley Field.

He never did get to build his dynasty. In fact, Dallas was dumped by the Cubs, but not before he unloaded most of the 1984 talent he assembled. Only

◆

three S's remained in 1989 from his NL East Division winners: Sandberg, Sanderson, and Sutcliffe.

Leaving the Cubs' front office, Green joined the Yankees as manager for the 1989 season. It was a gathering of egos with George Steinbrenner as owner and Dallas in the dugout. It lasted a half-season. Then Green was given the green light to go—elsewhere.

But Dallas Green left his legacy with the Cubs. He put some life in the moribund franchise and dragged them kicking and screaming into the 20th century.

**B. June 2, 1938, Kent, Ohio    BR TR    6'2"    183 lbs.**

# GENE MICHAEL

Courtesy of Chicago Cubs

A ballclub is often a reflection of its manager. During the mid-1980s the Cubs were dull and lifeless. Eugene Richard Michael was the Cub manager from June 1986 to September 1987.

His was a familiar face in the Cubs dugout during

◆

that span. He sat with a frown and seldom moved. It was as if someone had planted a statue of Calvin Coolidge, the president (not Calvin Coolidge McLish, the pitcher), in that spot.

Nicknamed "Stick," the cadaverous Michael replaced Jim Frey and compiled a 114–124 record before being bounced by front office boss Dallas Green. Nothing much happened during Michael's short reign in Cubby blue.

He once emerged from the shady shadows of the Cub dugout to argue a call with an umpire. He spun the ump's cap around and drew plaudits from Cub partisans. It was probably his lone day in the Wrigley Field sun.

The silver-haired Michael had served two terms as one of George Steinbrenner's parade of Yankee pilots. He replaced Bob Lemon as manager and later was replaced by Bob Lemon.

The Stick also stuck around as a Yankee general manager, scout, coach, and minor league manager. Today, he's back with the Yankees in some capacity. It changes with Steinbrenner's moods.

Michael, a 52-year-old native of Kent, Ohio, broke in with the Pittsburgh Pirates as a shortstop in 1966 after eight arduous seasons in the bush leagues. He was sent to the Los Angeles Dodgers the following season as part of a package for Maury Wills.

He began his long association with the Yankees Nov. 30, 1967, when his contract was purchased from the Dodgers. Michael became part of Yankee lore when he combined with Bobby Murcer and Thurman Munson to hit three consecutive homers in one inning on Aug. 10, 1969.

The often asked trivia question is: Name the three "M" Yankees to hit three straight homers in one inning. Most experts figure it's Murcer and Munson, plus Mickey Mantle. Few would guess Michael, with his lifetime average of .229 and only 15 homers.

♦

**B. July 30, 1957, Detroit, Mich.    BL TL    6′4″    195 lbs.**

# STEVE TROUT

Courtesy of Chicago Cubs

After swimming against the tide for six sinking seasons, Steven Russell Trout finally found the pot of gold at the end of the rainbow. Trout went fishing in free agent waters before the Cubs landed him for five years at $4.5 million.

The 1984 season was a lucky season for "Rainbow" Trout, who showed his true colors with a brilliant 13–7 record and a 3.41 ERA. Prior to 1984 the enigmatic left-hander floundered with murky marks.

It wasn't until he hooked up with Cub pitching coach Billy Connors that Trout scaled the mound heights. Connors baited Trout. He worked on his mechanics, his work habits, his attitude, his confidence, and gave him a sense of pride and purpose.

Trout, 27, is the son of former Detroit Tigers' pitching great Paul "Dizzy" Trout, a right-hander, who won 170 and lost 161 games during 15 fun-filled seasons.

Combined with Steve's 88–92 record, the Trouts rank as the all-time winning father-son pitching duo

♦

in baseball history with a 258–253 record. The two Trouts top the Cleveland Indians' combo of Jim Bagby, Sr., (127–89) and Jim Bagby, Jr., (97–96) and a 224–185 mark.

The elder Trout died in 1972 when Steve was 14. "My dad told me when I was a kid, 'Whatever you do, have fun.' So I try to have fun," said Steve, who grew up in South Holland, a Chicago suburb. "People are going to cheer you or boo you. All you can do is the best you can."

Despite a brilliant sinkerball, Trout's best often wasn't good enough. Signed out of high school by the crosstown White Sox in the first round of the free agent draft on June 8, 1976 (the eighth player selected overall), Trout posted a 1–3 record with the Sarasota Sox.

After whistle stops at Appleton, Knoxville, and Des Moines, the lanky, shaggy-haired blond reported to the White Sox late in 1978 and was unbeatable with a 3–0 record.

The following season Trout was 11–8, joining a left-handed quartet of Tex Wortham (14–14), Ken Kravec (15–13), and Ross Baumgarten (13–8). The four were hailed as the pitching wave of the future. But it didn't last for long. As a power pitcher, Rainbow had neither willpower nor staying power. The next three years Trout and his sinkerball sunk to 9–16, 8–7, and 6–9 seasons.

The Sox swapped Trout and sore-armed reliever Warren Brusstar to the Cubs for pitchers Randy Martz and Dick Tidrow, plus infielders Scott Fletcher and Pat Tabler on Jan. 26, 1983. The deal looked like a steal for the Sox.

Connors received a call the following day from General Manager Dallas Green. "I just traded for Steve Trout," said Dallas. "He's your pet project. You've got to get through to him."

The pudgy pitching coach was handed quite a

project. He patted him on the back. He kicked his butt. He induced Trout to go back to his basic pitches. But the Cubs were losers and Rainbow went to pot.

His 10–14 record was deserving. Trout completed only 1 of 32 starts, rarely got to the seventh inning, and allowed 217 hits in 180 innings. He wound up in the bullpen and was forgotten and abandoned by managers Lee Elia and Charlie Fox.

Jim Frey, the Cubs' fresh new manager for 1984, remembered Trout only vaguely from his American League days. "Good fastball and wild . . . or something like that," said Frey.

For a fellow whose promise always outweighed his production, it appeared to be Trout's final chance to stick with a big league club. Steve visited Connors in Florida prior to spring training and was warned by him.

"If you came down here to screw around, get on a plane and go home," said Connors. "I'm tired of your BS. You have a wife and baby to work for." Trout worked on Nautilus and started to eat better than in his vegetarian days. He got up to 205 pounds.

His big day came on April 13. It was the Cubs' home opener against the New York Mets and their highly touted rookie, 19-year-old Dwight Gooden. A crowd of 33,436 assembled at frigid Wrigley Field.

At the conclusion, it was a complete success for Trout, who went the route in an 11–2 Cub rout. The lefty was in command of his sinker and had the Mets beating the ball into the ground. "It was just a thing of being patient with him," said Connors. "We all go through a war. Some guy's turn comes, some don't."

Trout's best pitching performance was a 3–0 triumph over the Mets in the first game of a doubleheader at Shea Stadium on July 29. Trout recorded 16 ground outs as the Cubs took a double bite out of the Big Apple. It was Steve's first shutout since 1980, raising his record to 10–5.

♦

Down the stretch, the Cubs hit a snag—a five-game losing streak. It was up to Trout to bail them out.

Steve came through with a seven-hit, 8–1, complete game victory over the Cardinals in the opener of a doubleheader on September 23 at Busch Stadium. Dennis Eckersley completed the sweep with a 4–2 triumph and the Cubs reduced their magic number to one. The next day Rick Sutcliffe provided the clincher.

Manager Frey nominated Trout to pitch the second game of the National League championship playoffs against the Padres on October 2 at Wrigley Field. Trout proved a whale of a choice, going eight and one-third innings in a 4–2 victory. After walking Kevin McReynolds with one out in the ninth, Frey relieved Trout and Lee Smith got the final two outs.

That brought a smile to Connors. "He made me really proud. It's all a part of growing up. People mature at different ages," said Billy.

From then on it was all downstream for Trout. Maturity? He missed one start after falling off a bicycle. Trout also went on the disabled list with a sore elbow. Steve's 1985 record fell to 9–7 and plummeted to 5–7 in 1986.

By then, Connors was gone. Trout had to sink or swim on his own. Somehow he managed back-to-back shutout wins. GM Dallas Green offered Trout as trade bait and the Yankees bit the hook.

On July 12, 1987, Trout was traded to New York for three pitchers—Bob Tewksbury, Rich Scheid and Dean Williams. The Cubs also collected some of George Steinbrenner's cash.

Despite Trout's peculiarities, the deal wasn't popular with Cub fans, who saw it as unloading another big salary. It didn't help any when Tewksbury was ineffective with the Cubs, posting an 0–4 record. The other two pitchers never made it to the big leagues.

◆

Steve was also 0–4 with the Yankees and soon found himself floundering with the Mariners where he closed out his career, for the time being, with an 88–92 record. Reportedly, he has been attempting to make a comeback in the majors.

**B. Aug. 3, 1954, Oakland, Calif.   BR TR   6'2"   195 lbs.**

# DENNIS ECKERSLEY

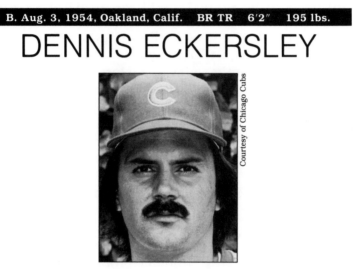

Courtesy of Chicago Cubs

If anyone qualified as the hard luck man on the 1984 Cub pitching staff it was Dennis Eckersley. With just a few breaks, his 10–8 record could easily have been in the vicinity of 15–3.

It was a long trail of professional experience that eventually led Eckersley to the Friendly Confines. Upon graduating from high school, he was picked by the Indian organization in the third round of the free agent draft on June 6, 1972.

Sent to the Tribe's farm team in Reno of the California League, Dennis did not show unusual promise his first season, but improved his record to

♦

12–8 in 1973. Upon advancing to San Antonio of the Texas League the following year, he responded with a 14–3 mark and a league-leading 163 strikeouts.

By now Eckersley looked ready for the majors and he was. Spending all of 1975 with Cleveland, he came through with a 13–7 record and a sparkling 2.60 ERA. The next two seasons he posted 13 and 14 wins, and in 1976 he averaged nine strikeouts per game, fanning 200 in 199 innings.

The greatest outing of Eckersley's career so far came on May 30, 1977, when he no-hit the Angels 1–0. Yet 10 months later—on March 30, 1978—he was swapped to the Red Sox with catcher Fred Kendall for pitchers Rick Wise and Mike Paxton, third baseman Ted Cox, and catcher Bo Diaz.

Eckersley's first two years with Boston are among his best to date as a starter. He was 20–8 in 1978 and 17–10 the next year, posting a 2.99 ERA both seasons. Thereafter, however, his performance at the Hub was largely disappointing. His earned run average expanded and it became a constant struggle to reach the .500 mark. In his last year and a half with the Red Sox, he began having shoulder problems as well.

Meanwhile, by early 1984, veteran Cub first baseman Bill Buckner had been supplanted by Leon Durham and desired to move on to greener pastures. On May 25 he was traded to the Red Sox for Eckersley and minor league infielder Mike Brumley. At the time, the new Cub pitcher was 4–4 with a 5.01 ERA.

Although Dennis said, "I want to go in there and show I can pitch," his start in Chicago was hardly an auspicious one. He lost five of his first six decisions as a Cub. He allowed only seven earned runs in his first three appearances over 22 innings but came away with an 0–2 ledger. It seemed that Cub power was conspicuous by its absence whenever he took the hill. Eckersley then started getting bombed himself. By All-Star time, he was 2–5 with a 4.88 ERA.

◆

Then came the turnaround. From the All-Star break to the end of the regular season, Dennis made 15 starts and was 8–3 with a 2.06 ERA. He lasted at least into the seventh inning in 13 of the 15 starts, while allowing two earned runs or less in 12 of his last 13 outings. On September 23 his 4–2 victory over the Cardinals in St. Louis clinched a tie for the division championship.

Eckersley won one more after that to finish 10–8 as a Cub, while his overall mark of 14–12 was his best since 1979. His 3.03 ERA was second only to Rick Sutcliffe among Cub starters. He suffered five losses by one run and another two by two runs. On August 9 he shut out the Expos on four hits through nine innings, only to go decisionless as the Cubs lost 1–0 in the 10th inning.

Sadly, in his lone appearance in the playoffs, Eckersley was ineffective. Having never faced the Padres before, he was slugged for nine hits and five earned runs in five and one-third innings, getting tagged with the loss as San Diego beat the Cubs 7–1.

On Nov. 28, 1984, he signed a three-year contract with the Cubs, saying, "It's a great organization and a great city to play in."

Early in 1985, Eckersley went on the disabled list with a sore shoulder. But he came back in time to lead the team in victories with an 11–7 record. His pin-point control was astounding as he allowed only 19 walks, while whiffing 117 batters.

But everything went sour the following season. He was dogged mainly by a lack of offense. It seemed as if his teammates marched to the plate with wet noodles instead of bats.

Consequently Eckersley's record fell to 6–11, his worst ever. Cub trademaker Dallas Green apparently was fooled. Two days after April Fool's day in 1987 Green made his worst move, sending Eckersley to the Oakland Athletics along with infielder Dan Rohn for three nobodies.

◆

For the record they were outfielder David Wilder, infielder Brian Guinn and pitcher Mark Leonette. None ever got to wear a Cub uniform. It was quite apparent Green was unloading a big salary for a bunch of celery.

Dennis immediately became a menace with the A's. He was switched from starter to reliever and emerged as the top Fireman in both leagues. Eckersley started with 16 saves in 1987.

The 1988 season found Eckersley rushing out of the bullpen to earn a whopping 45 saves with a solid 2.63 earned run average. That was enough to finish second to Minnesota's Frank Viola in the Cy Young balloting.

Somehow, the A's lost the World Series to the inferior Los Angeles Dodgers. But even an earthquake couldn't stop them in 1989. With Eckersley in control, the A's swept the San Francisco Giants in four games. Another good guy got away.

**B. Dec. 4, 1957, Jamestown, La.   BR TR   6'6"   235 lbs.**

# LEE SMITH

Courtesy of Chicago Cubs

♦

Lee Smith was easily the Cubs' most effective fireman throughout most of the 1980s. He brought no trickery to his relief work, as did Bruce Sutter with his split-fingered fastball; Smith merely reared back and dared the batters to hit his heat.

Smith built his powerful body by milking cows, slopping hogs, and carrying firewood on his family's farm in Louisiana. He built his reputation as a basketball and baseball star at Castor (La.) High School. As a pitcher, he won 15 in a row and then lost his final game, a one-hitter, at Castor. That performance alone had him mentally prepared for his future as a Cub.

Smith was scouted by Buck O'Neill of the Cubs, who signed Ernie Banks two decades earlier. But Smith wanted a college education and envisioned himself bouncing a basketball in the NBA. He sought out former Braves' slugger Joe Adcock, who resides in nearby Coushatta, La. Adcock advised him to get a college education and go for baseball afterwards.

In addition, a physician told Smith he wouldn't last more than two seasons in the NBA because of his "jumper's knees." It seemed that Smith had grown so fast that he didn't have much cartilage left in his knees.

Smith attended Northwestern Louisiana and was selected by the Cubs in the second round of the 1975 draft. But his climb to the majors was strewn with too many minor league losses.

While at Midland in the Texas League, Smith was introduced to relief pitching by manager Randy Hundley, the Cubs' former Rebel with a cause. Randy, a thinking man's catcher, wanted Smitty to concentrate on every batter.

Hundley brought Smith into a game with the bases loaded and one out and told him not to let anyone score. "I struck out the two guys and it turned my career around," said Smith.

In spring training the next season, Hundley was catching Smith. "We were fooling around on the

♦

sidelines and I started throwing sidearm," revealed Smith. Hundley asked Smith to throw sidearm in a game and his career blossomed.

He was promoted to Wichita of the American Association in 1980. There he had 63 strikeouts in 90 innings and saved 15 games. Smith was brought up by the Cubs late in the season and he showed the right stuff, fanning 17 in 22 innings and winning two games.

The strike-shortened 1981 season was almost a total loss for Smith and the Cubs. Although Smith struck out 50 in 67 innings, he earned only one save and had a 3–6 record.

By the time 1982 rolled around, the Cubs were under new ownership and Lee was just another guy named Smith as far as Dallas Green and Lee Elia were concerned.

Somehow, Smith showed enough to stick, but was in and out as a starter and reliever. It wasn't until July that Elia turned Smith loose exclusively in the bullpen.

From July 8 on, Smith appeared in 35 games and allowed only four earned runs for a 0.96 ERA and 15 of his 17 saves. He retired an amazing 19 straight batters in one stretch from August 18 to September 7, with eight of them strikeout victims.

He was 0–4 as a starter and 2–5 overall with a 2.69 ERA. In addition, Smith hit a homer on July 5, striking the right field foul pole in Atlanta off veteran knuckler Phil Niekro. It was his first big league hit.

The affable, gentlemanly giant was gaining recognition around the league as a premier reliever. Such hitters as Pete Rose and Mike Schmidt of the Phillies and Al Oliver of the Expos started tossing accolades.

Best of all, Smitty was recognized as a genuine talent by Dallas Green, even though Lee wasn't weaned in the Phillies' farm system. Smith was now deemed a suitable successor to Sutter.

The 1983 season saw Smitty surpass Sutter in saves, 29 to 21. Lee's total topped the National League,

◆

as did his stingy 1.65 ERA. But his 103 innings pitched weren't enough for him to qualify for the ERA title.

His 91 strikeouts ranked him second among bull-pen artists to the Phillies' Al Holland, who had 100. Somehow, Smith still had trouble winning clutch games, as attested by his 4–10 won-lost record.

But he was good enough to make the National League squad for the annual All-Star Game at Comiskey Park. The American League finally burst out of its slumber, ending its 11-game losing streak by shelling the National League 13–3.

Lee pitched one inning, gave up two runs, one unearned, but salvaged some respect for the Cubs. The highlight of the evening as far as Cub fans were concerned was the moment Smith encountered Ron Kittle, the White Sox rookie *wunderkind.*

Suddenly, in the eighth inning it was Cubs versus the White Sox. Kittle at the plate and Smitty on the mound. All eyes were focused on the pair. The cre-scendo of the crowd was deafening.

It was strength against strength as Smitty fired a fastball and Kittle went fishing for strike three. Smitty had Kittle over a kettle.

Lee picked up where he left off in 1984. Although his earned run average ballooned to 3.65, he won 9 and dropped 7, while saving 33 games, only 4 shy of Sutter's Cub record.

In one contest, on August 2, the Cubs were leading 3–2 in the ninth inning with the Montreal Expos. Runners stood on first and third with one out.

Pete Rose slammed a line drive up the middle. The ball bounced off Smith's shoulder and shortstop Dave Owens caught it in midair and threw to first for a game-ending double play. That game came to be known as the "immaculate deflection" and proved that somebody up there liked the Cubs.

But the Padres prayed harder and Smith didn't escape unscathed in the National League playoffs

♦

when the pesky Steve Garvey poked Lee's smokeball for a game-winning homer to tie the ill-fated series at two games each.

Although the Cubs ceased to excel after 1984, Smith continued to do so. Lee duplicated his 33 saves, shaved his ERA down to 3.04, and whiffed 112 batters in just 98 innings—his best season to date. Nine times he struck out the side. On four occasions he fanned five in one game, an impressive total for a relief pitcher. In his first six appearances, April 9–30, 1985, he notched up five saves while fanning 18 batters and allowed only one earned run in 10⅔ innings.

In 1986, Lee's nine wins tied him with Scott Sanderson for the club leadership while his 31 saves made him the first NL hurler to save 30 or more games for three consecutive seasons. Between July 29 and August 25 he enjoyed a scoreless streak of 16⅔ innings. The Cubs, who won only 70 games all season, were 42–17 in games that Smith finished, so his continued value to the team was obvious. For his heroic efforts, Lee received Chicago Player of the Year Honors from the Chicago Baseball Writers.

The next season, Lee increased his save count to 36, one short of the Cub record set by Bruce Sutter in 1979. But, his record fell to 4–10 and he allowed 15 more hits in six fewer innings than in 1986. It appeared to some that he was becoming overripe. On Dec. 8, 1987, he was traded to the Red Sox for pitchers Calvin Schiraldi and Al Nipper.

The general opinion was that the Cubs were swindled. History has borne this out, as Schiraldi and Nipper achieved practically nothing in Chicago. On the other hand, Smith, while not quite as imposing as he was with the Cubs, has continued to breeze his fast one by anxious batters in the AL. He saved 29 games for Boston in 1988 and 25 in 1989. His saves for save opportunities percentage of .833 (25 for 30) was third in the league last season. He fanned 96 batters in 70⅔

♦

innings en route to a 6–1 record to add to his saves. Lifetime, Lee is 50–57 with—much more importantly—234 saves. His 180 saves in a Cub uniform are a team record and likely to remain so for at least a few more years.

**B. Jan. 5, 1957, Kansas City, Mo.   BR TR   6'0"   160 lbs.**

# BOBBY DERNIER

The best way to describe the Cubs' acquisition of Bobby Dernier is a case of highway robbery. Although only a "throw-in" as part of a trade, Bobby's brand of center field in 1984 was something Cub fans had not witnessed in a generation.

Prior to donning Cub pinstripes, Dernier was essentially a baseball nobody. Making his professional debut with Spartanburg of the West Carolina League in 1978, he moved to Helena of the Pioneer League and finished the season there. His combined batting average for 75 games was .263.

With Peninsula of the Carolina League the following year, he batted .291 and led the league in stolen bases with 77. Moving up to Reading of the Eastern

◆

**115**

League in 1980, Dernier hit .299 with a league-leading 71 steals. Late in the season the Phillies gave him a cup of coffee in the big time.

Then it was out to Oklahoma City for the final grooming at the Triple A level in the American Association. There it was much of the same for Bobby—a .302 average and 72 stolen bases to lead the league. At the end of the year, he made another brief appearance at Philadelphia.

It now looked as if Bobby was ready for the majors, but in 1982 he was somewhat disappointing in his first full season with the Phillies. Although his 42 stolen bases made a good impression, Bobby's .249 average and 21 RBI did not. The next season, with far fewer at bats, he dropped to .231. He appeared in one game as an outfield defensive replacement during the pennant playoffs and once as a pinch runner in the World Series, scoring one run.

Dernier was still an unknown on March 27, 1984, when he, outfielder Gary Matthews, and pitcher Porfi Altimarino were swapped to the Cubs for catcher Mike Diaz and pitcher Bill Campbell. It was Matthews the Cubs were after; the other two appeared to be just excess baggage the Phillies wanted to unload. When it was announced that Dernier would be starting in center field, the talented but moody Cub outfielder Mel Hall remarked, "I can't see Bob Dernier taking my job. I don't think he's qualified and I don't mind telling anyone that." But by the arrival of opening day, Dernier was in center field while Hall was moved to right en route to being exiled to Cleveland.

Bobby quickly proved himself the Cubs' best center fielder since the days of Andy Pafko, if not beyond. He covered all of his turf and then some, made breathtaking running catches, and displayed a strong, accurate throwing arm. When Keith Moreland returned to right field on a full-time basis after Hall was traded, the Cub outfield was solidified.

◆

The best surprise, however, was that Dernier began hitting with authority, proving himself an ideal leadoff man for the big guns to blast across the plate. On May 24, 1984, he went 5 for 5 and stole two bases in a 10–7 victory over the Braves at Wrigley Field. He legged out two infield hits and had a bloop single to left. It was the first five-hit game by a Cub since Ivan DeJesus did it against the Cardinals on April 22, 1980.

Interviewed after the game, Bobby commented nonchalantly, "It was a lucky day. It was the kind of day you sleep well after." Possibly it was not all luck, either, for on May 30 he had a repeat 5-for-5 outing in a 6–2 triumph over the Braves at Atlanta, stealing two bases and scoring three runs.

At the halfway point of the season, Dernier was batting a cool .316. Although his hitting tailed off thereafter, he still finished with a respectable .278 average, 149 hits, and 94 runs scored, seventh in the league. When he stole his 33rd base on July 21, sportswriters who had obviously not read their history books asserted that he "broke the Cubs record for stolen bases by a center fielder, surpassing Adolfo Phillips's 32 in 1966." Forgotten were Bill Lange's 41 in 1899 and Jimmy Slagle's 40 in 1902, but Bobby soon had the club position record all to himself. When he finished the year with 45 thefts—eighth in the league—it was the most by a Cub player since Johnny Evers swiped 46 back in 1907. Moreover, it was the general consensus that Dernier was worth having in the lineup solely for his defensive ability, even if he had batted only .200 and not stolen a base.

During the postseason pennant playoffs Bobby surprised everyone—including himself—by belting a first inning homer (he had only three during the regular season) in the series opener October 2. In the Wrigley Field boxes his radiant wife beamed on national TV. Dernier had become only the second player in National League playoff history to homer in his first at bat, the

♦

other being Joe Morgan of the Reds in 1972. For the rest of the day he had a walk and a run scored in the third, and a double, a walk, and another run in a six-run fifth. The Cubs went on to trounce the Padres, 13–0, to set a record for most runs scored in a playoff game.

More heroics followed in game two, October 3. Leading off the first inning with a single, he made a daring dash from first to third on Ryne Sandberg's grounder, then scored on a grounder by Gary Matthews. In the fourth inning, after forcing Steve Trout, he stole second and scored on Ryne Sandberg's double as the Cubs went on to win 4–2.

Sadly, it was to be the last hurrah that season for both Dernier and the Cubs. For the final three games at San Diego, Bobby collected only one more hit, a single, and stole no more bases as the Padres swept at home to win the pennant. Nevertheless, no one can deny that he gave Cub fans plenty to cheer about in 1984.

That season was the apex of Bobby's career. Beset with injuries the following two seasons, he spent three weeks on the disabled list in 1985 with a foot injury, and five weeks in 1986 with a torn rotator cuff in his right shoulder. His batting averages tailed off to .254 and .225. However, he continued to excel on the basepaths, stealing 31 bases in 1985 and 27 in 1986. On July 30, 1986, he stole three bases against the Mets in a 4–3 Cub victory.

In 1987 Dernier batted .317 with 8 homers, both career highs, but he came to bat only 199 times. On October 27, he filed for free agency, signing with his old team, the Phillies, on December 7.

But the magic of 1984 has yet to return for Bobby. During the past two seasons at Philadelphia, he has been a part-time, oft-injured player, batting .289 in 1988 and only .171 last year. Going into the upcoming season, he is a .255 lifetime hitter with 23 home runs and 152 RBI.

♦

**B. July 5, 1950, San Fernando, Calif.   BR TR   6'2"   205 lbs.**

# GARY MATTHEWS

Courtesy of AU Sports

It took only one season for "Sarge" to earn his stripes. Gary Nathaniel Matthews led the Cubs' charge to the top with his leadership and bubbly effervescence.

In addition, he uncorked 19 game-winning hits, scored 101 runs, coaxed a league-leading 103 walks, and seemed to be in the middle of every crucial Cub rally.

As a youngster, growing up in the San Fernando Valley near Los Angeles, Matthews used to sneak into Dodger Stadium. "I used to change the ticket stubs, slip in behind somebody, do whatever I had to do," said Matthews. "Now, I get to play left field when I get to Dodger Stadium. It really cracks me up."

Matthews was selected by the San Francisco Giants, the 17th player grabbed in the free agent draft on June 7, 1968. But he didn't rate highly with Giant officials because of his trouble with breaking pitches.

Only Gary and batting instructor Hank Sauer kept the faith. "I can see us now," recalled Matthews,

♦

"Garry Maddox and I, swinging at slider after slider thrown by Don McMahon."

Sauer patiently stood at the batting cage, gazing at Gary in the winter mornings in the Arizona Instructional League. "I had so many blisters from hitting sliders, I thought it was the easiest pitch to hit," Matthews later said.

Sauer's patience paid off as his pupil powdered the pill at Phoenix in 1972, batting .313 with 21 homers and 108 RBI. That earned him a promotion to the Giants, where he batted .300 and was named National League Rookie of the Year in 1973.

After five solid seasons as a Giant, Matthews declared himself a free agent and signed a fat contract with Ted Turner's Atlanta Braves on Nov. 17, 1976. "I didn't get along with Turner," confessed Matthews.

"I spoke out on things that were happening around me. When the Braves sent Bob Horner to the minors, I said 'How in the world can you send him down after he hit 30 homers last year?'"

As a reward the Braves replied, "OK, we'll just sit your butt down on the bench and watch you sulk." "That gave me a bad reputation. I learned a lesson. If somebody isn't playing, I'll just keep quiet."

At about that time Matthews taught the Cubs a lesson in hustle. There was a game in Atlanta in 1979. The Cubs had two on base with Dave Kingman up. Kong slammed a high drive to right that was labeled a homer.

Matthews raced to the chicken wire fence, leaped à la Michael Jordan, and snared the ball at the tip of his glove. The force of the drive almost knocked Gary over the fence.

Even though Matthews had a no-trade clause in his contract, he welcomed the deal that sent him to the Philadelphia Phillies for pitcher Bob Walk on March 25, 1981. He enjoyed a .301 season under manager Dallas Green and a .289 year under manager Pat Corrales.

♦

But 1983 was an off season for Gary. His average plummeted to .258 and he was platooned. He finally responded in October, hitting .429 with 3 homers and 8 RBI to wreck the Dodgers in the National League playoffs and get the Phillies into the World Series.

In spring training of 1984, the downtrodden Cubbies were having their problems. Errors were turning the games into a boot camp.

After watching the Cubs lose 11 in a row, with fly balls dropping everywhere in left, center, and right, new manager Jim Frey called the Cubs' outfield play "stinko."

Finally, on March 27, General Manager Green sent reliever Bill Campbell and minor leaguer Mike Diaz to the Phillies for Matthews, center fielder Bob Dernier, and someone named Porfi Altamirano.

Dernier proved to be the Cubs' first bona fide center fielder in eons. And Matthews? "We needed a screamer, a holler guy, a leader," said Green. "When I realized I could get him from the Phillies, I couldn't say yes fast enough. He talks when it's time to talk, and he produces when it's time to produce."

Matthews was off to a great start with the Cubs, hitting safely in 13 of the first 15 games, batting .360 on 18 hits in 50 trips with 16 walks. He had a 4-for-5 effort against the Reds on May 15, and was 4 for 4 against the Astros on August 14.

But Matthews reached his zenith on September 23 when the Cubs needed him the most. They were mired in a five-game losing streak when they took on the Cardinals in a doubleheader before 46,083 fans at Busch Memorial Stadium.

The Cubs swept the Cards 8–1 and 4–2 and reduced their magic number to one. Sarge drove in the winning runs in both games. He socked a three-run double in the first game and walloped a two-run homer in the second.

The following night the Cubs clinched the National League East Division title, beating the Pirates 4–1

◆

behind Rick Sutcliffe, who reeled off his 14th victory in a row.

Again, it was the effervescent Matthews who was sipping and spraying champagne after picking up his 19th game-winning RBI of the season.

Mid-season knee surgery reduced The Sarge to a platoon player in 1985. He will still a swinger at bat, but a defensive liability in the outfield. Although playing part-time, Matthews somehow led the Cubs in homers with 21 the following year.

GM Dallas Green began cleaning house and Matthews found himself in a Seattle uniform midway through 1987. He was traded to the Mariners for Hartnett. No. Not Gabby Hartnett. It was a pitcher named David Hartnett, who never even sipped a cup of coffee with the Cubbies.

Without Matthews the spark was gone and the Cubs faded from contention. After retiring, Gary set up shop in Chicago and did some announcing gigs on cable TV.

**B. May 2, 1954, Dallas, Tex.   BR TR   6'0"   200 lbs.**

# KEITH MORELAND

Courtesy of Chicago Cubs

◆

Keith Moreland was the Cubs' regular right fielder when they won the Eastern Division title in 1984. Breaking into the pros with Spartanburg in 1975, Moreland also saw service in Peninsula, Reading, and Oklahoma City in the Phillies' farm chain. At the end of the 1978 season he was brought up to the Phillies, but failed to get a hit in his only two trips to the plate. The following year it was back to Oklahoma City, where he batted .302, tied for the league lead in doubles with 34, hit 20 home runs, and knocked home 109 runs.

Keith was then recalled to Philadelphia, and this time it looked as if he was ready for the majors. Playing 62 games in 1980, he batted .314. However, when he dropped to .255 the next season, the Phillies soured on him.

On Dec. 8, 1981, the Cubs traded Mike Krukow and cash to the Phillies for Moreland, and pitchers Dickie Noles and Dan Larson. Keith was the Cubs' springtime wonder in early 1982, batting .356 through May 21 with 8 homers and 33 RBI. At one point he hit safely in 18 of 19 games, and on May 7 he hit two homers while driving home seven runs in a 12–6 triumph over Houston.

His fielding, however, was something else. Stationed in the catcher's box at the outset, he committed repeated throwing errors. By mid-May he was relocated to right field. His bat soon went silent, as he finished at .261 with 15 homers and 68 RBI.

In 1983 Moreland was a far more consistent hitter. Hovering near the .300 level the entire season, Keith finished with a .302 mark to lead the team while upping his homer count to 16 and his RBI to 70. His 11 game-winning RBI were tied with Ron Cey for the club lead.

Despite his impressive showing, Moreland had no guarantee of a job the following spring. When outfielders Gary Matthews and Bobby Dernier were virtually stolen from the Phillies, the regular patrol was Matthews in left, Dernier in center, Mel Hall in right, and Moreland wherever there was an empty spot in the lineup.

During the early part of the season Keith was on the bench just as often as he was on the field. Several times he asked to be traded. After Hall was dealt to Cleveland June 13, Moreland was again the regular right fielder, but he had only 29 RBI at the season's halfway point.

In the meantime, the Cubs of 1984 had developed a pattern of producing a new superhero every month. In May it was first baseman Bull Durham; the following month Ryne Sandberg reached unprecedented heights. Starting in July, pitcher Rick Sutcliffe emerged as an overpowering stopper.

In August it was Moreland's turn to rise to the occasion. Some of the other Cubs—Durham, Dernier, Davis—were beginning to wear out in the heat, but Keith, who had seen far less action, became the Cubs' "gun of August."

From August 1 through August 8 he went 18 for 34 for a .529 average with four homers, 15 RBI, four game-winning hits, and two game-tying hits. Game-winner number one was a grand slam homer that provided the margin in a 4–3 victory over Montreal August 5, with the Wrigley Field fans giving Keith a standing ovation. The bat he used, incidentally, was one he had borrowed from Sandberg.

Then the Mets, trailing the Cubs by only half a game, arrived in Chicago for a crucial four game series. The first contest saw Moreland collect the game-winner in a 9–3 romp. In the second game, the opener of an August 7 doubleheader, his three-run homer was the catalyst for a six-run fifth inning in an 8–6 Cub win. After tremorous chants of "Keith, Keith" from the standing-room-only crowd, he emerged from the dugout waving his cap in acknowl-

◆

edgment. After the game he said, "I just don't know how to handle that sometimes, I mean, I don't want to be showing anybody up on their [the Mets'] team, but you do want to thank the fans."

The nightcap was highlighted by a bench-clearing brawl when Moreland was hit on the thigh by a pitch from Met starter Ed Lynch. Keith charged the mound, roll-blocked Lynch, and the fight was on. "I just went out there to get my point across," said Moreland. "It's part of the game of baseball. I have no hard feelings against anybody." Gary Matthews added, "The Mets can't intimidate us. We don't have the big head. But they're not budging us from the dish either."

Keith was clearly the man of the hour as the demoralized Mets never again seriously challenged the Cubs' lead. Moreland, meanwhile, remained as hot as the weather. Keith finished with a .360 average for August with five homers, 32 RBI, and eight game-winning hits, earning him the National League Player of the Month honors.

Although Moreland cooled off in September, he still finished with a .279 average, 16 homers to tie his personal best, and a career high 80 RBI, most of them in key situations. His 11 game-winning hits were third on the club to Gary Matthews's 19 and Bull Durham's 14.

In the playoffs Keith batted .333, but with no especially significant hits, as the Padres defeated the Cubs in five games. He did, however, give Cub fans an unforgettable thrill in the championship opener.

The Padres had the bases loaded with two out in the fourth inning when Carmelo Martinez slapped a sinking liner over Ryne Sandberg's head. Moreland charged in, dived, and picked the ball off the tops of the Wrigley Field grass blades. Had Keith missed it, he could well have ended up a goat, but he did not, and the Cubs went on to win 13–0.

◆

Although the Cubs sagged to fourth in 1985, it could not be blamed on Moreland, who had by far the best season of his career. Hitting like a hurricane, the hustling Texan led the Cubs in batting with .307 and RBI with 106. He had 12 game-winning hits, 16 game-tying hits, and an 18-game hitting streak from September 12 through 29. With men in scoring position, he was .338 for the season.

In 1986 Keith tailed off a bit, but still batted .271 while again leading the club in RBI with 79, and in game-tying hits with 13. His 13 assists in the outfield were the most by a Cub since Jose Cardenal had 14 in 1975.

Switched to third base in 1987, Moreland was no Brooks Robinson defensively, as indicated by his 28 errors and .934 fielding average. Never an outstanding gloveman wherever he was positioned, Keith looked awkward and uncomfortable at third base. Although he socked a career high 27 homers and drove home 88 runs, his days as a Cub were numbered. On Feb. 12, 1988, he and infielder Mike Brumley were swapped to the Padres for pitchers Rich "Goose" Gossage and Ray Hayward.

After a disappointing season at San Diego, Keith divided 1989 between the Tigers and the Orioles, batting .278 as a semi-regular. At the end of the season, he announced his retirement from baseball, leaving behind a career .279 average with 1,279 hits, 121 homers, and 674 RBI. While not a gifted natural, Moreland was a classic example of a journeyman ballplayer who got a lot of mileage out of effort and determination.

♦

# 1985–86

# 1984 Stars in Decline

B. Feb. 16, 1948, Tacoma, Wash.   BR TR   5′9″   185 lbs.

## RON CEY

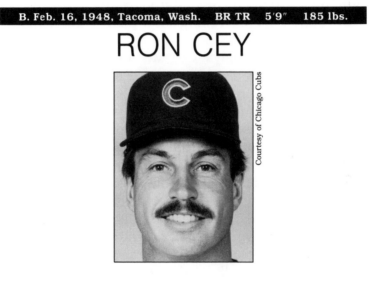

Courtesy of Chicago Cubs

It took "the Penguin" to help the Cubs out of the deep freeze. Ronald Charles Cey didn't exactly swing the hottest bat, but 187 RBI in two Cub seasons proved he was no cold stiff.

♦

As a member of the Los Angeles Dodgers, Cey would waddle into Wrigley Field and rattle the fences. For instance, on June 6, 1974, the young third baseman drove in seven runs with two homers and a single to lead LA to a 10–0 romp over the hapless Cubbies.

Whenever the Dodgers visited Chicago, the sun was always shining and the wind was blowing out.

Cey, a Dodger mainstay for 11 solid seasons, was obtained from LA on Jan. 20, 1983, for Cub farmhands Dan Cataline, an outfielder, and Vance Lovelace, a pitcher.

A native of Tacoma, Washington, Ron was originally selected by the New York Mets in the 24th round of the draft on June 6, 1966. He preferred an education and attended Washington State and Western Washington before signing with the Dodgers' organization in 1968.

In his playing days, Cey was a powerful 5'9" and 185 pounds. His short arms and stocky legs, combined with his pronounced waddle earned him the nickname "Penguin."

Third base had been an enigma for 16 seasons since the Dodgers deserted Brooklyn for the West Coast. In 1972, Cey became the club's 43rd third baseman after destroying Pacific Coast pitching, batting .328 at Spokane and .329 at Albuquerque with two year totals of 55 homers and 226 RBI.

His offensive production and defensive work ended the long search. For the next decade Cey was a big gun in the middle of the Dodger lineup. His 228 homers is a Dodger record, LA variety.

Cey hit .350 with one homer and drove in six runs to share 1981 World Series MVP honors with Pedro Guerrero and Steve Yeager. But Dodger management thought the team was getting too long in the tooth.

Steve Garvey at first, Davey Lopes at second, Bill Russell at short, and Cey at third, had remained

♦

intact for 10 seasons, setting an all-time record for an infield quartet.

Lopes was dispatched to Oakland and then wound up with the Cubs. Garvey, demanding a zillion, was the big cheese in the 1982 re-entry draft of free agents. The Cubs engaged in an all-out bidding war and lost to the Padres. They then set their sights on Cey.

Ron looked forward to playing at Wrigley. His wife, Fran, is a native Chicagoan, and the park seemed ideal for his hitting talent. Little did he realize he was no longer facing Cub pitching.

At the outset of the 1983 season everything went wrong. The first six weeks were the most brutal of his career. The weather was horrible, he hurt his shoulder, and the team was losing, losing, losing. Cey was an easy target for the boobirds. "Booing is something with which you try not to concern yourself," sighed Cey. "If you're booed on the road, it means the other team's fans respect you. But if you're booed at home, it's hard to feel good about it."

Eventually Cey shook his slump and emerged as the Cub clean-up hitter. He led the team in RBI with 90 and shared homer leadership with Jody Davis at 24, while batting .275. At third base Cey displayed good instincts and a strong arm, but lacked mobility.

Cey's second Chicago season was eventful and painful. He was charged with an error in the opener against the Giants at Candlestick Park and then played the next 60 games before committing another one.

The Penguin had his customary power at the plate, but his average remained frozen—.200 and below. After hitting his sixth career grand slam against the Giants at Wrigley Field on May 8, Ron started thumping out of his slump.

Then he injured his right wrist when he was hit by the Cardinals' Ralph Citarella on June 23. X-rays

♦

showed nothing wrong, but he was bothered by pain throughout the rest of the season.

Sore wrist and all, Cey led the 1984 Cubs in homers (25) and RBI (97) and even got his average up to .240. Ron had a lot to say with the Cubs making the playoffs.

Ron also had a lot to Cey in the Cubs setback in 1985. He hit 22 homers, but that was offset by his league-leading 21 errors at third base. Where he used to waddle, he started to crawl.

Cey's lack of mobility, combined with Larry Bowa's lack of range at shortstop, made the left side of the infield vulnerable to any sharply hit grounder.

Although he still packed some punch at the plate, the 1986 season found Cey dividing the bag with former Dodger teammate Davey Lopes. Cey was sent to the Oakland A's for infielder Luis Quinones on Jan. 30, 1987. Cey spent a half season as designated hitter before drawing his release.

Cey's short stay with the Cubs was productive: 84 homers and 286 RBI. And Cub fans can always recall their 1984 NL East Division all-animal infield of the Bull (Leon Durham), the Ryno (Ryne Sandberg), the Bow-Wow (Larry Bowa) and the Penguin (Ron Cey).

**B. May 3, 1946, Providence, R.I.   BR TR   5'9"   170 lbs.**

# DAVEY LOPES

Courtesy of AU Sports

On April 26, 1985, Davey Lopes hit his 100th homer in the National League. It's ironic that Lopes's milestone was in a Chicago uniform, because he was always a millstone to the Cubs.

As a Dodger, Lopes usually had the Cubs on the ropes during his long career. He enjoyed his best day at the Cubs' expense at Wrigley Field one August day in 1974 when he had five hits, including three homers.

And who could forget his ninth inning grand slam homer at Dodger Stadium off Cub relief ace Bruce Sutter. Now, after a dozen seasons as a tormentor, the former Dodger captain is a Cub.

Lopes was acquired from the Oakland A's on Aug. 31, 1984, and in his first at bat he doubled off the Phillies' Steve Carlton. Lopes batted .235 (4 for 17) during his September stint.

Lopes, who made his name as a second baseman, didn't see much action there with the Cubs. That's Ryno territory.

♦

But Lopes saw action just about everywhere else in 1985. He played all the other infield spots, the outfield, and came off the bench to pinch-hit or pinch-run. And did he ever run! Can you imagine a scrub stealing 47 bases? In addition, Davey batted a solid .284.

Lopes was batting .299 with 17 stolen bases midway through the 1986 season. But the Cubs were getting shelled in the late innings and needed a left-handed reliever. He was dealt to the Houston Astros for pitcher Frank DiPino. In Houston his average dwindled to .235 and he stole only eight bases.

With his playing time diminished, Lopes joined the Texas Rangers as a coach. He concluded his playing career with 557 stolen bases, 10th on the all-time list.

**B. Dec. 6, 1945, Sacramento, Calif.   BB TR   5'10"   155 lbs.**

# LARRY BOWA

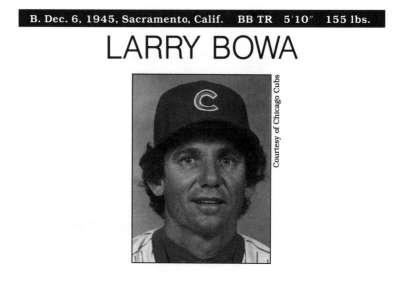

Courtesy of Chicago Cubs

♦

Although Larry Bowa is of Polish descent, he was once carried on a list of outstanding American athletes of Italian ancestry. He was the Cubs' shortstop from 1982 to 1985 with uneven success.

Bowa began his career with Spartanburg of the Western Carolina League in 1966, batting .312 and playing 26 consecutive errorless games at shortstop. From there he moved up the ladder to San Diego, Bakersfield, Reading, and finally Eugene (Ore.) of the Pacific Coast League—the Phillies' Triple A team. After batting .287 at Eugene in 1969, Bowa was deemed ready for Philadelphia.

Larry was given the Phillies' starting job at shortstop in 1970 and he never relinquished it. He immediately gained a reputation as a stereotyped "good field, no hit" shortstop.

In 1971 he set a major league record for highest fielding average (.9869) and fewest errors (11) by a shortstop, only to see them wiped out by the Tigers' Eddie Brinkman the following year. In 1972 Bowa himself lowered his error count to nine and lifted his fielding average to .9874, both of which remain the National League standards. It was in that year also that he won his first of two Gold Glove Awards.

In the seasons that followed, Larry continued to be a smooth fielder while improving his batting skills, reaching a career high of .305 in 1975. He also proved himself a clever baserunner, stealing 39 bases in 1974, the year he was the starting shortstop on the National League All-Star squad.

Critics, however, regarded Bowa as an Astroturf hitter, whose average was fattened by the bounce of ersatz grass. They further maintained that his high fielding averages and miniscule boot totals were due to lack of range as much as fielding skill. At the time, the Phillie brass was apparently satisfied with his work and he kept his job.

Then, on Jan. 27, 1982, the Cubs traded Ivan

♦

DeJesus to the Phillies for Bowa and infielder Ryne Sandberg. Although Sandberg proved to be a worthy investment, some could see no logic in replacing the 29-year-old DeJesus with a Bowa who was pushing 37.

With the Cubs floundering miserably and Bowa hitting only .186 by June 8, he became the object of many a jeer and catcall from fans who longed for DeJesus. Larry then turned things around. He ended up batting .360 for the month of June.

However, it was a roller coaster thereafter, and he finished at .246. His 29 RBI were the lowest among the starting lineup and he had but one game-winning RBI. He had also slowed down at shortstop and was no longer a basestealing threat.

In 1983 Larry raised his batting average to .267, collected hit No. 2,000 of his major league career, and led the league in fielding average for the seventh time. Appointed team captain, he shared a title once held by such hallowed names as Charlie Grimm, Phil Cavarretta, and Ron Santo.

Captain or not, Bowa was clearly the weakest link at the plate in the Cub chain as the 1984 season unfolded. Time after time he came to the plate with runners on base and failed to drive them in, prompting cynical fans to label him "the constrictor." At one stretch he came to bat 130 times without driving home a run. He had but two RBI after June 30. More and more frequently, he found himself benched in favor of Dave Owen and Tom Veryzer.

On July 18 Bowa asked the Cubs to "play me or release me." Later, in regard to Jim Frey, he said, "He doesn't like me, so he doesn't play me." Frey replied, "He's not producing, that's all."

The situation reached its nadir at Wrigley Field August 3. Having spotted the Expos a 5–0 lead, the Cubs had rallied for two in the sixth, two in the seventh, and so far one in the eighth to knot up the

♦

score. Larry was at bat with the bases loaded and the squeeze play on. Unfortunately, Bowa missed on the bunt attempt, causing Keith Moreland to be cut down at the plate. Then, he bounced out to the pitcher to end the inning.

Worse was yet to come. In the top of the ninth, with the bases loaded and one out, Dan Driessen grounded a tailor-made double-play ball to Ryne Sandberg, who flipped to Bowa. Larry stepped on second for the force, then failed to get the ball from his glove as Max Venable crossed the plate with what became the winning run in a 6–5 heartbreaker.

Larry finished the season with a .224 average, no homers and 17 RBI. In fairness, Bowa's savvy was a big help. His experience and maturity provided psychological stability to a team largely composed of youths.

Bowa became a semi-regular in 1985. The Cubs brought up highly touted shortstop Shawon Dunston as Bowa's eventual successor. Most veterans take raw recruits under their wing, but Bowa refused to yield his position, acting like a brat.

Although Frey remained silent, third base coach Don Zimmer tore into Bowa. To make room for Dunston, Bowa was waived to the Mets late in the season, thus departing from the Cubs under a cloud.

In 72 games as a Cub, Bowa batted .246 with no homers and only 13 RBI. Bowa was also ineffective with the Mets, batting .105 in 14 games. His complete Cub career revealed Bowa as not much in the clutch. A player with only 102 RBI in 1,584 at bats is virtually nonproductive.

After drawing his release from the Mets, Larry was signed to manage Las Vegas of the Pacific Coast League in 1986, where he was fairly successful, winning 88 and losing 62. Although Bowa was on a roll with Las Vegas he crapped out as a major league manager.

♦

**135**

He was given the opportunity of piloting the San Diego Padres in 1987. But his frequent outbursts with umpires, management and his players led to his dismissal after the season. The Padres finished last with a 65–97 mark under Bowa, who later found a more suitable position as a coach with his beloved Phillies.

# Cubs Home Run Stats

Home run! No two words in the English language have inspired such colorful slang terms. There's circuit clout, round tripper, four-ply smash, tater, four-bagger, prodigious blow, four-sacker, bell-ringer, dinger, the long ball, and Elvis has left the building.

H is for homer and Cubs with nicknames such as Hack, Hawk, Hank, Handy Andy, plus Hartnett have hammered quite a few. S is for Sweet Swinging Billy, Swish and Santo and Sandberg.

And, finally, there's Mr. Cub—Ernie Banks.

All of the above have put the Cubs in the forefront of the four-bagger.

Did you know the first homer in National League history was hit by a Cub? It happened on May 2, 1876. Second baseman Ross Barnes connected for an inside-the-park smash off pitcher Bill Cherokee in Cincinnati as the Cubs crushed the Reds 15–9.

Cub third baseman Ed Williamson hit 27 homers in 1884 to set a record unmatched until broken by a guy named Babe Ruth in 1919. Ruth, converted from a pitcher to an outfielder by the Boston Red Sox, hit 29 homers that season.

◆

Another Cub homer record was tied but never broken. Player-manager Cap Anson hit five homers in a period of two consecutive games (Aug. 5–6, 1884). That record was tied by future Cubs Billy Williams and Dave Kingman, among others.

Cubs' outfielder Frank "Wildfire" Schulte hit four grand slam homers in 1911, a mark that stood for decades, until Banks hit five slams in 1955. In addition, the Cubs set a league record by slugging nine grand slam homers in 1929.

The league record for homers in a season is 56 by rotund Hack Wilson of the 1930 Cubs. That was the same season Wilson established a mark that will probably never be broken. Wilson drove in 190 runs. Not even such big boppers as the Babe, Lou Gehrig, Hank Greenberg, or Jimmy Foxx came close.

Perhaps the most famous homer against the Cubs came in the third game of the 1932 World Series at Wrigley Field. In the fifth inning, Ruth allegedly called his famous shot by pointing toward the right-center field bleachers and then rocketing the ball in the exact spot.

One of the least known homer feats occurred at Wrigley Field on June 25, 1937. Cub outfielder Augie Galan became the first switch-hitter in big league history to hit a homer left-handed and right-handed in the same game.

And the best known Cub homer was hit 5:37 p.m., Sept. 28, 1938, at Wrigley Field. The Cubs and Pittsburgh Pirates were in a dogfight for the pennant. They came to Chicago in first place and departed as runners-up.

The Pirates were a half-game ahead when they clashed on a dark, dank, dreary day. The shadows of evening fell on the field as the teams were tied 5–5 in the ninth inning. The umpires conferred and decided to call the contest at the conclusion of the inning.

With two outs in the ninth, Cub player-manager

♦

Gabby Hartnett strode to the plate in the dusk. Gabby swung and missed twice off Pirates' ace reliever Mace Brown. And then it happened. Hartnett connected and sent the ball into the left field bleachers for a 6–5 Cub victory.

The victory put the Cubs in first to stay. Hartnett's historic blow has become renowned as the "Homer In The Gloamin'." It was the most memorable moment in Cubs history.

During the 1940s, a husky slugger named Bill Nicholson would grip the bat so hard one could see sawdust fallout. And when he swung and missed, fans would yell "Swish."

Swish was involved in one of the most unusual feats in a game against the Dodgers at Wrigley Field in 1943. Phil Cavarretta homered off the right field foul pole and the ball bounced back on the field. The umpire checked the ball and gave it back to Dodger pitcher Johnny Allen.

On the next delivery, Swish swung and hit the ball out of the park. The result? One ball for two homers on two pitches by one pitcher.

Nicholson set a record of sorts by swatting six homers within 40 hours. He homered once Friday evening, once Saturday and four times on Sunday. The dates were July 21–23, 1944. Nicholson had hit four homers in a row at New York's old Polo Grounds.

And when he stepped up to the plate the next time with the bases loaded, Giants' manager Mel Ott ordered Nicholson to be walked intentionally to bring home one run instead of four.

The Cubs enjoyed another historic moment at the Polo Grounds. Cub hitters Eddie Waitkus and Marv Rickert hit back-to-back, inside-the-park homers on June 23, 1946—a league feat never equaled.

And did you know that nobody has ever homered off the present-day scoreboard at Wrigley Field—except for golfer Sam Snead, who used a 2-iron to smack

♦

a golf ball off the facade? Pittsburgh's Roberto Clemente and "Swish" Nicholson came closest. Clemente stroked the ball to the left of the scoreboard onto Waveland Avenue. Nicholson sent one onto Sheffield Avenue that struck a building and bounced off the hood of a southbound car.

During the 1950s, a new hero appeared by the name of Hammering Hank Sauer. He entered the record books by hitting 14 homers off the Pirates in one season. Sauer also hit three homers in one game off Curt Simmons of the Philadelphia Phillies for a 3–0 victory.

Simmons then went into the Army. But when he returned, Sauer hit three more off the fast-balling lefty in one game. Imagine, six homers off one pitcher in two games.

Although many consider Wrigley Field a bandbox and home run haven, the park boasts the longest dimensions down the foul lines, 355 feet in left and 353 in right.

The longest homer was struck by Dave Kingman when he was a member of the New York Mets on April 14, 1976. It was a wind-swept afternoon and King Kong sent the ball soaring some 600 feet. The ball struck the porch of the third house on Kenmore Avenue and was caught on the rebound by a fan named Richard Keiber. The Cub pitcher, incidentally, was Tom Dettore.

Over the years, the most productive homer slugger at Wrigley Field was Ernie Banks with 290. Rounding out the top seven are Billy Williams, 231; Ron Santo, 212; Hank Sauer, 118; Gabby Hartnett, 115; Hack Wilson, 109; and Bill Nicholson, 91.

Among the visiting players, Willie Mays holds a 54 to 50 lead over Hank Aaron and Mike Schmidt.

For opening-day thrills, none matched the 1969 opener. That's when Wonderful Willie Smith provided the Cubs punch in the pinch. The date was April 8,

1969. Don Money of the Phillies and Banks had already hit two homers each and Philly was leading 6–5 in the bottom of the 11th inning.

Randy Hundley singled with one out and Cub manager Leo Durocher sent in Smitty as a pinch-hitter. While swinging in the on-deck circle, Smith hit himself in the hip with the bat. It really stung.

Several minutes later, Smitty stung the ball, drilling it high and deep into the right field bleachers for a 7–6 Cub victory that sent a crowd of 40,796 home delirious.

Although Hartnett's homer in the dark was tops, Cub fans rated Bank's 500th homer as the greatest moment in Cub history. It was another dreary, rainy afternoon on May 12, 1970.

The Atlanta Braves were in town when Ernie came to bat with two out in the second inning. On the one-one count, Braves pitcher Pat Jarvis served again, only to see it sail into the left field bleachers for Ernie's 500th. He was given a standing ovation as he crossed the plate, and the Cubs went on to win 4–3 in 11 innings.

Modern-day Cub fans rate the Ryne Sandberg vs. Bruce Sutter encounter as tops for thrills. The Cubs met the St. Louis Cardinals at Wrigley Field before a packed house and a national TV audience on June 23, 1984.

The Cardinals raced to a 7–1 lead, but the Cubbies clawed back like grizzly bears to chop the St. Louis lead to 9–8. Sandberg came to bat in the bottom of the ninth and homered off Cardinals relief ace Sutter to tie the score.

When the contest went into extra innings, the Cardinals rallied for two runs and an 11–9 lead. But lightning struck again in the same spot. Ryno rifled the ball in the same spot with a man aboard off Sutter to tie the score in the bottom of the 11th. The Cubs went on to win 12–11.

◆

And, finally, here's one for trivia buffs. Which major league ballpark did Lou Gehrig homer in first? Yankee Stadium? Guess again. On June 26, 1920, Lane Technical High School of Chicago was playing the High School of Commerce from New York for the inter-city baseball championship at Wrigley Field.

The score was 8–8 and Commerce had the bases loaded when Gehrig, a high school junior, stepped up and hit the first ball pitch over the right field wall for a 12–8 victory.

The home run is the ultimate thrill in baseball. Over the years, Cub players have given their fans plenty of these thrills. Following is a list of various records and statistics on Cub home runs.

♦

# Home Run Leaders

| Rank | Player | Total | Rank | Player | Total |
|------|--------|-------|------|--------|-------|
| 1. | Ernie Banks | 512 | 33. | Augie Galan | 59 |
| 2. | Billy Williams | 392 | 33. | Jerry Morales | 59 |
| 3. | Ron Santo | 337 | 35. | Rogers Hornsby | 58 |
| 4. | Gabby Hartnett | 231 | 36. | Bill Dahlen | 57 |
| 5. | Bill Nicholson | 205 | 36. | Stan Hack | 57 |
| 6. | Hank Sauer | 198 | 38. | Dale Long | 55 |
| 7. | Hack Wilson | 190 | 39. | Vic Saier | 53 |
| 8. | Ryne Sandberg | 139 | 40. | Roy Smalley | 52 |
| 9. | Leon Durham | 138 | 41. | Ralph Kiner | 50 |
| 10. | Andy Pafko | 126 | 42. | Frank Demaree | 49 |
| 11. | Jody Davis | 122 | 42. | Riggs Stephenson | 49 |
| 12. | Rick Monday | 106 | 44. | Hank Leiber | 48 |
| 13. | Keith Moreland | 100 | 44. | Gary Matthews | 48 |
| 14. | Jimmy Ryan | 99 | 44. | Bill Serena | 48 |
| 15. | Cap Anson | 97 | 47. | Heinie Zimmerman | 47 |
| 15. | Jim Hickman | 97 | 48. | Chuck Klein | 46 |
| 17. | Andre Dawson | 95 | 48. | Adolfo Phillips | 46 |
| 18. | Dave Kingman | 94 | 50. | Shawon Dunston | 44 |
| 19. | Phil Cavarretta | 92 | 51. | Bobby Murcer | 43 |
| 20. | Frank Schulte | 91 | 51. | Walt Wilmot | 43 |
| 21. | Randy Jackson | 88 | 53. | Jerry Martin | 42 |
| 22. | Ron Cey | 84 | 54. | Tommy Burns | 40 |
| 22. | Moose Moryn | 84 | 54. | Abner Dalrymple | 40 |
| 24. | George Altman | 83 | 54. | Bill Lange | 40 |
| 25. | Bill Buckner | 81 | 57. | Joe Pepitone | 39 |
| 26. | Randy Hundley | 80 | 58. | Hack Miller | 38 |
| 27. | Kiki Cuyler | 79 | 58. | Lee Walls | 38 |
| 27. | Fred Pfeffer | 79 | 60. | Gene Baker | 37 |
| 29. | Dee Fondy | 66 | 60. | Billy Herman | 37 |
| 30. | Jose Cardenal | 61 | 62. | Eddie Miksis | 34 |
| 30. | Charlie Grimm | 61 | 62. | Cy Williams | 34 |
| 30. | Ed Williamson | 61 | | | |

◆

**143**

| Rank | Player | Total | Rank | Player | Total |
|------|--------|-------|------|--------|-------|
| 64. | Cliff Heathcote | 33 | 85. | George Gore | 24 |
| 64. | King Kelly | 33 | 86. | George Decker | 23 |
| 64. | Clyde | | 86. | Frank Thomas | 23 |
| | McCullough | 33 | 88. | Barry Foote | 22 |
| 67. | Bobby Thomson | 32 | 88. | Glenn Beckert | 22 |
| 67. | Manny Trillo | 32 | 88. | Dom Dallessandro | 22 |
| 69. | Woody English | 31 | 88. | Mel Hall | 22 |
| 69. | Bill Madlock | 31 | 88. | Hal Jeffcoat | 22 |
| 71. | Babe Herman | 30 | 88. | Peanuts Lowrey | 22 |
| 71. | Andre Thornton | 30 | 88. | Rip Russell | 22 |
| 71. | Sammy Taylor | 30 | 95. | Silver Flint | 21 |
| 74. | Rip Collins | 29 | 96. | Mark Grace | 20 |
| 74. | Joe Tinker | 29 | 96. | Larry Biittner | 20 |
| 76. | Andre Rodgers | 28 | 96. | Lou Brock | 20 |
| 76. | Bob Speake | 28 | 96. | Frank Chance | 20 |
| 78. | Johnny Callison | 27 | 96. | Harry Chiti | 20 |
| 78. | Ray Grimes | 27 | 96. | Billy Cowan | 20 |
| 78. | Bob O'Farrell | 27 | 96. | Carmen Fanzone | 20 |
| 81. | Jim King | 26 | 96. | George Grantham | 20 |
| 81. | George Mitterwald | 26 | 96. | Danny Green | 20 |
| 83. | Bob Neeman | 25 | 96. | Billy Jurges | 20 |
| 83. | Rafael Palmeiro | 25 | | | |

# Year-By-Year Leaders

| Year | Player | Total |
|------|--------|-------|
| 1876 | Paul Hines | 2 |
| 1877 | No homers | 0 |
| 1878 | Frank Hankinson–John Remsen–Joe Start | 1 |
| 1879 | Silver Flint–John Peters–Ed Williamson | 1 |
| 1880 | George Gore | 2 |
| 1881 | Tom Burns | 4 |
| 1882 | Silver Flint | 4 |
| 1883 | King Kelly | 3 |
| 1884* | Ed Williamson | 27 |
| 1885* | Abner Dalrymple | 11 |
| 1886 | Cap Anson | 10 |
| 1887 | Fred Pfeffer | 16 |
| 1888* | Jimmy Ryan | 16 |
| 1889 | Jimmy Ryan | 17 |
| 1890* | Walt Wilmot | 14 |
| 1891 | Walt Wilmot | 11 |
| 1892 | Jimmy Ryan | 10 |
| 1893 | Bill Lange | 8 |
| 1894 | Bill Dahlen | 15 |
| 1895 | Bill Lange | 10 |
| 1896 | Bill Dahlen | 9 |
| 1897 | Bill Dahlen | 6 |
| 1898 | Bill Lange | 6 |
| 1899 | Sam Mertes | 9 |
| 1900 | Sam Mertes | 7 |
| 1901 | Topsy Hartsel | 7 |
| 1902 | Joe Tinker–Charles Dexter | 2 |
| 1903 | Johnny Kling | 3 |
| 1904 | Frank Chance | 6 |
| 1905 | Frank Chance–Joe Tinker–Bill Maloney | 2 |

| Year | Player | Total |
|------|--------|-------|
| 1906 | Frank Schulte | 7 |
| 1907 | Frank Schulte–Johnny Evers | 2 |
| 1908 | Joe Tinker | 6 |
| 1909 | Frank Schulte–Joe Tinker | 4 |
| 1910** | Frank Schulte | 10 |
| 1911** | Frank Schulte | 21 |
| 1912** | Heinie Zimmerman | 14 |
| 1913 | Vic Saier | 14 |
| 1914 | Vic Saier | 18 |
| 1915 | Cy Williams | 13 |
| 1916** | Cy Williams | 12 |
| 1917 | Larry Doyle | 6 |
| 1918 | Max Flack | 4 |
| 1919 | Max Flack | 6 |
| 1920 | Dave Robertson | 10 |
| 1921 | Max Flack–Ray Grimes | 6 |
| 1922 | Ray Grimes | 14 |
| 1923 | Hack Miller | 20 |
| 1924 | Gabby Hartnett | 16 |
| 1925 | Gabby Hartnett | 24 |
| 1926* | Hack Wilson | 21 |
| 1927* | Hack Wilson | 30 |
| 1928* | Hack Wilson | 31 |
| 1929 | Rogers Hornsby–Hack Wilson | 39 |
| 1930*** | Hack Wilson | 56 |
| 1931 | Rogers Hornsby | 16 |
| 1932 | John Moore | 13 |
| 1933 | Gabby Hartnett–Babe Herman | 16 |
| 1934 | Gabby Hartnett | 22 |
| 1935 | Chuck Klein | 21 |
| 1936 | Frank Demaree | 16 |
| 1937 | Augie Galan | 18 |
| 1938 | Rip Collins | 13 |
| 1939 | Hank Leiber | 24 |
| 1940 | Bill Nicholson | 25 |
| 1941 | Bill Nicholson | 26 |
| 1942 | Bill Nicholson | 21 |
| 1943* | Bill Nicholson | 29 |
| 1944** | Bill Nicholson | 33 |

♦

| Year | Player | Total |
|------|--------|-------|
| 1945 | Bill Nicholson | 13 |
| 1946 | Bill Nicholson–Phil Cavarretta | 8 |
| 1947 | Bill Nicholson | 26 |
| 1948 | Andy Pafko | 26 |
| 1949 | Hank Sauer | 27 |
| 1950 | Andy Pafko | 36 |
| 1951 | Hank Sauer | 30 |
| 1952** | Hank Sauer | 37 |
| 1953 | Ralph Kiner | 28 |
| 1954 | Hank Sauer | 41 |
| 1955 | Ernie Banks | 44 |
| 1956 | Ernie Banks | 28 |
| 1957 | Ernie Banks | 43 |
| 1958** | Ernie Banks | 47 |
| 1959 | Ernie Banks | 45 |
| 1960** | Ernie Banks | 41 |
| 1961 | Ernie Banks | 29 |
| 1962 | Ernie Banks | 37 |
| 1963 | Ron Santo–Billy Williams | 25 |
| 1964 | Billy Williams | 33 |
| 1965 | Billy Williams | 34 |
| 1966 | Ron Santo | 30 |
| 1967 | Ron Santo | 31 |
| 1968 | Ernie Banks | 32 |
| 1969 | Ron Santo | 29 |
| 1970 | Billy Williams | 42 |
| 1971 | Billy Williams | 28 |
| 1972 | Billy Williams | 37 |
| 1973 | Rick Monday | 26 |
| 1974 | Rick Monday | 20 |
| 1975 | Andy Thornton | 18 |
| 1976 | Rick Monday | 32 |
| 1977 | Bobby Murcer | 27 |
| 1978 | Dave Kingman | 28 |
| 1979** | Dave Kingman | 48 |
| 1980 | Jerry Martin | 23 |
| 1981 | Bill Buckner–Leon Durham | 10 |
| 1982 | Leon Durham | 22 |
| 1983 | Ron Cey–Jody Davis | 24 |

♦

| Year | Player | Total |
|------|--------|-------|
| 1984 | Ron Cey | 25 |
| 1985 | Ryne Sandberg | 26 |
| 1986 | Jody Davis–Gary Matthews | 21 |
| 1987 | Andre Dawson | 49 |
| 1988 | Andre Dawson | 24 |
| 1989 | Ryne Sandberg | 30 |

*Led National League
**Led both leagues
***National League record

# Home Run Leaders By Decades (Top Ten)

## 1870s

| | | |
|---|---|---|
| 1. | Paul Hines | 2 |
| 1. | John Peters | 2 |
| 3. | Cap Anson | 1 |
| 3. | Ross Barnes | 1 |
| 3. | Silver Flint | 1 |
| 3. | Frank Hankinson | 1 |
| 3. | Cal McVey | 1 |
| 3. | John Remsen | 1 |
| 3. | Joe Start | 1 |
| 3. | James White | 1 |
| 3. | Ed Williamson | 1 |

## 1880s

| | | |
|---|---|---|
| 1. | Fred Pfeffer | 70 |
| 2. | Cap Anson | 67 |
| 3. | Ed Williamson | 60 |
| 4. | Jimmy Ryan | 48 |
| 5. | Abner Dalrymple | 40 |
| 6. | Tommy Burns | 33 |
| 6. | King Kelly | 33 |
| 8. | George Gore | 24 |
| 9. | Silver Flint | 20 |
| 10. | Hugh Duffy | 19 |

## 1890s

| | | |
|---|---|---|
| 1. | Bill Dahlen | 57 |
| 2. | Jimmy Ryan | 46 |
| 3. | Walt Wilmot | 43 |
| 4. | Bill Lange | 40 |
| 5. | Cap Anson | 28 |
| 6. | George Decker | 23 |
| 7. | Sam Carroll | 14 |
| 8. | Bill Everett | 13 |
| 9. | Milachi Kittredge | 12 |
| 10. | Bill Hutchison | 11 |

## 1900s

| | | |
|---|---|---|
| 1. | Joe Tinker | 22 |
| 2. | Frank Chance | 17 |
| 2. | Frank Schulte | 17 |
| 4. | Johnny Kling | 13 |
| 5. | Danny Green | 10 |
| 6. | Solly Hofman | 9 |
| 7. | Topsy Hartsel | 7 |
| 7. | Sam Mertes | 7 |
| 7. | Harry Steinfeldt | 7 |
| 10. | Johnny Evers | 5 |
| | Jimmy Sheckard | 5 |
| | Jimmy Ryan | 5 |

♦

# 1910s

| | | |
|---|---|---|
| 1. | Frank Schulte | 74 |
| 2. | Vic Saier | 53 |
| 3. | Heinie Zimmerman | 47 |
| 4. | Cy Williams | 34 |
| 5. | Jimmy Archer | 15 |
| 5. | Tommy Leach | 15 |
| 7. | Max Flack | 13 |
| 8. | Jimmy Sheckard | 12 |
| 9. | Fred Merkle | 9 |
| 10. | Larry Doyle | 7 |

# 1920s

| | | |
|---|---|---|
| 1. | Hack Wilson | 121 |
| 2. | Gabby Hartnett | 81 |
| 3. | Rogers Hornsby | 39 |
| 4. | Hack Miller | 38 |
| 5. | Charlie Grimm | 35 |
| 5. | Riggs Stephenson | 35 |
| 7. | Cliff Heathcote | 33 |
| 8. | Kiki Cuyler | 32 |
| 9. | Ray Grimes | 27 |
| 10. | Bob O'Farrell | 26 |

# 1930s

| | | |
|---|---|---|
| 1. | Gabby Hartnett | 149 |
| 2. | Hack Wilson | 69 |
| 3. | Augie Galan | 55 |
| 4. | Frank Demaree | 49 |
| 5. | Kiki Cuyler | 47 |
| 6. | Chuck Klein | 46 |
| 7. | Billy Herman | 32 |
| 8. | Babe Herman | 30 |
| 9. | Rip Collins | 29 |
| 10. | Stan Hack | 28 |

# 1940s

| | | |
|---|---|---|
| 1. | Bill Nicholson | 200 |
| 2. | Andy Pafko | 78 |
| 3. | Phil Cavarretta | 51 |
| 4. | Stan Hack | 29 |
| 5. | Hank Sauer | 27 |
| 6. | Clyde McCullough | 24 |
| 7. | Dom Dallessandro | 22 |
| 7. | Peanuts Lowrey | 22 |
| 9. | Lou Stringer | 17 |
| 10. | Babe Dahlgren | 16 |
| | Bob Scheffing | 16 |

# 1950s

| | | |
|---|---|---|
| 1. | Ernie Banks | 238 |
| 2. | Hank Sauer | 171 |
| 3. | Randy Jackson | 88 |
| 4. | Moose Moryn | 82 |
| 5. | Dee Fondy | 66 |
| 6. | Dale Long | 55 |
| 7. | Ralph Kiner | 50 |
| 8. | Andy Pafko | 48 |
| 9. | Bill Serena | 47 |
| 10. | Roy Smalley | 40 |

# 1960s

| | | |
|---|---|---|
| 1. | Ernie Banks | 269 |
| 2. | Ron Santo | 253 |
| 3. | Billy Williams | 239 |
| 4. | George Altman | 71 |
| 5. | Randy Hundley | 58 |
| 6. | Adolfo Phillips | 46 |
| 7. | Andre Rodgers | 28 |
| 8. | Jim Hickman | 26 |
| 9. | Frank Thomas | 23 |
| 10. | Lou Brock | 20 |
| | Billy Cowan | 20 |

♦

# 1970s

| | | |
|---|---|---|
| 1. | Billy Williams | 143 |
| 2. | Rick Monday | 106 |
| 3. | Ron Santo | 84 |
| 4. | Dave Kingman | 76 |
| 5. | Jim Hickman | 71 |
| 6. | Jose Cardenal | 61 |
| 7. | Jerry Morales | 54 |
| 8. | Bobby Murcer | 43 |
| 9. | Joe Pepitone | 39 |
| 10. | Bill Madlock | 31 |

# 1980s

| | | |
|---|---|---|
| 1. | Ryne Sandberg | 139 |
| 2. | Leon Durham | 138 |
| 3. | Jody Davis | 122 |
| 4. | Keith Moreland | 100 |
| 5. | Andre Dawson | 95 |
| 6. | Ron Cey | 84 |
| 7. | Bill Buckner | 51 |
| 8. | Gary Matthews | 48 |
| 9. | Shawon Dunston | 44 |
| 10. | Rafael Palmeiro | 25 |

◆

# Grand Slam Homers

## (1876-1899)

| Date | | Player | Team Pitcher | Inning | Site |
|------|---|--------|--------------|--------|------|
| 1882 | June 20 | Larry Corcoran | Worcester— | | |
| | | | Richmond | (9) | H |
| 1884 | June 21 | Fred Pfeffer | Braves—Whitney | (1) | H |
| 1886 | Sept. 8 | Jimmy Ryan | Giants—Welch | (6) | H |
| 1884 | Aug. 14 | King Kelly | Buffalo—Seard | (2) | H |
| 1889 | May 9 | Addison Gumbert | Pirates—Conway | (4) | H |
| 1889 | Aug. 17 | Jimmy Ryan | Washington— | | |
| | | | Sullivan | (6) | H |
| 1890 | May 8 | Howard Earl | Reds—Viau | (6) | H |
| 1890 | June 26 | Howard Earl | Dodgers—Lovett | (1) | H |
| 1890 | Aug. 16 | Tommy Burns | Pirates—Phillips | (5) | H |
| 1890 | Aug. 16 | Milachi Kittredge | Pirates—Phillips | (5) | H |
| 1890 | Sept. 8 | Elmer Foster | Pirates—Anderson | (1) | H |
| 1893 | July 11 | Bill Lange | Washington— | | |
| | | | Duryea | (1) | H |
| 1893 | Sept. 3 | Milachi Kittredge | Baltimore—Mullane | (5) | H |
| 1893 | Sept. 10 | Jiggs Parrott | Washington—Maul | (4) | H |
| 1894 | July 29 | Walt Wilmot | Reds—Flynn | (8) | A |
| 1894 | Aug. 1 | Cap Anson | Cardinals—Mason | (5) | H |
| 1894 | Aug. 11 | Charlie Irwin | Cleveland—Cuppy | (5) | H |
| 1895 | May 20 | Asa Stewart | Phillies—Carsey | (8) | H |
| 1895 | Aug. 24 | Jimmy Ryan | Washington— | | |
| | | | Anderson | (1) | A |
| 1896 | May 18 | Bill Lange | Giants—Campfield | (6) | H |
| 1897 | June 29 | Jimmy Ryan | Louisville—Frazer | (2) | H |
| 1899 | Aug. 28 | Bill Everett | Giants—Gettig | (5) | H |

◆
**152**

# (1900–1909)

| Date | | Player | Team Pitcher | Inning | Site |
|---|---|---|---|---|---|
| 1902 | Aug. 4 | Frank Chance | Phillies—White | (12) | A |
| 1904 | Aug. 17 | Jack O'Neil | Braves—Fisher | (4) | A |
| 1905 | June 25 | Bill Maloney | Reds—Harper | (5) | H |
| 1908 | June 6 | Johnny Kling | Braves—Young | (3) | A |
| 1908 | Sept. 12 | Johnny Kling | Cardinals—Lush | (12) | A |

# (1910–1919)

| Date | | Player | Team Pitcher | Inning | Site |
|---|---|---|---|---|---|
| 1911 | June 3 | Frank Schulte | Giants—Marquard | (8) | H |
| 1911 | July 4 | Frank Schulte | Reds—Keefe | (3) | H |
| 1911 | July 15 | Joe Tinker | Braves—Mattern | (7) | A |
| 1911 | July 18 | Frank Schulte | Braves—Tyler | (6) | A |
| 1911 | Aug. 16 | Frank Schulte | Braves—R. Brown | (4) | A |
| 1911 | Sept. 21 | Vic Saier | Phillies—Chalmers | (3) | H 2d G |
| 1913 | May 25 | Vic Saier | Cardinals—Steel | (1) | H |
| 1913 | Aug. 25 | Cy Williams | Dodgers—Rucker | (2) | H |
| 1913 | Sept. 6 | Vic Saier | Reds—Johnson | (1) | H |
| 1914 | Aug. 18 | Heinie Zimmerman | Dodgers—Ragan | (5) | H |
| 1918 | June 25 | Max Flack | Cardinals—Sherdel | (4) | H |

# (1920–1929)

| Date | | Player | Team Pitcher | Inning | Site |
|---|---|---|---|---|---|
| 1921 | Aug. 6 | Bob O'Farrell | Giants—Ryan | (4) | H |
| 1922 | June 27 | Elwood Wirts | Pirates—Glazner | (5) | H |
| 1922 | Sept. 16 | Hack Miller | Dodgers—Ruether | (1) | A |
| 1923 | June 12 | Hack Miller | Braves—F. Miller | (5) | H |
| 1923 | June 14 | Bob O'Farrell | Dodgers—Vance | (1) | H |
| 1923 | July 15 | Barney Friberg | Giants—Jonnard | (10) | A |
| 1924 | May 16 | George Grantham | Giants—Oeschger | (5) | H |
| 1924 | Aug. 9 | Jigger Statz | Braves—Benton | (10) | A |
| 1925 | Aug. 25 | Mandy Brooks | Phillies—Mitchell | (9) | A |
| 1926 | June 1 | Gabby Hartnett | Cardinals—Sherdel | (3) | H |

◆

**153**

| Date | | Player | Team Pitcher | Inning | Site |
|---|---|---|---|---|---|
| 1926 | Sept. 11 | Floyd Scott | Phillies—Knight | (7) | A |
| *1927 | May 1 | Clyde Tolson | Pirates—Kremer | (7) | H |
| 1928 | Apr. 19 | Hack Wilson | Reds—Luque | (2) | H |
| 1928 | July 3 | Riggs Stephenson | Cardinals—Haid | (9) | A |
| 1929 | Apr. 17 | Rogers Hornsby | Pirates—Fussell | (8) | H |
| 1929 | Apr. 18 | Charlie Grimm | Pirates—Petty | (3) | H |
| 1929 | May 17 | Hack Wilson | Reds—Donohue | (6) | H |
| 1929 | June 15 | Rogers Hornsby | Phillies—Collins | (7) | H |
| 1929 | June 18 | Hack Wilson | Cardinals—Haid | (5) | H |
| 1929 | June 29 | Charlie Grimm | Cardinals—Sherdel | (1) | A |
| 1929 | July 1 | Riggs Stephenson | Cardinals—Haines | (1) | A |
| 1929 | Aug. 26 | Norm McMillan | Reds—Ehrhardt | (8) | H |
| 1929 | Sept. 17 | Kiki Cuyler | Dodgers—Vance | (5) | H |

# (1930–1939)

| Date | | Player | Team Pitcher | Inning | Site |
|---|---|---|---|---|---|
| 1930 | Apr. 29 | Les Bell | Pirates—Kremer | (3) | H |
| 1930 | June 16 | Charlie Grimm | Giants—Hubbell | (9) | A |
| 1930 | Aug. 22 | Gabby Hartnett | Giants—Parmelee | (8) | H |
| 1931 | June 30 | Rogers Hornsby | Phillies—Dudley | (5) | A |
| *1931 | Sept. 13 | Rogers Hornsby | Braves—Cunningham | (11) | H |
| 1931 | Sept. 27 | Vince Barton | Pirates—Brame | (7) | H |
| 1933 | July 20 | Babe Herman | Phillies—Liska | (8) | H |
| 1933 | July 23 | Harvey Hendrick | Phillies—Collins | (10) | H |
| 1933 | Sept. 23 | Gabby Hartnett | Reds—Kolp | (6) | H |
| 1934 | May 18 | Tuck Stainback | Phillies—Holley | (3) | A |
| 1934 | June 22 | Chuck Klein | Giants—Castleman | (4) | H |
| 1935 | July 27 | Gabby Hartnett | Reds—Freitas | (4) | H |
| 1935 | Sept. 4 | Augie Galan | Phillies—Bivin | (8) | H |
| 1936 | May 16 | Phil Cavarretta | Phillies—Johnson | (8) | A |
| 1937 | May 5 | Frank Demaree | Phillies—Sivess | (6) | A |
| 1937 | June 29 | Billy Herman | Cardinals—Harrell | (7) | A |
| 1937 | Aug. 28 | Clay Bryant | Braves—Gable | (10) | A |
| 1938 | May 24 | Augie Galan | Dodgers—Mungo | (4) | A |
| 1938 | Sept. 14 | Gabby Hartnett | Braves—Fette | (3) | A |
| 1939 | June 22 | Augie Galan | Braves—Errickson | (2) | H |
| 1939 | Sept. 12 | Hank Leiber | Braves—Posedel | (1) | H |

*Pinch-hitter

◆
**154**

# (1940–1949)

| Date | Player | Team Pitcher | Inning | Site |
|---|---|---|---|---|
| 1940 Apr. 26 | Bill Nicholson | Reds—Thompson | 1 | H |
| 1940 June 30 | Jim Gleeson | Reds—Walters | 5 | A |
| 1940 July 5 | Rip Russell | Cardinals—Doyle | 5 | A |
| 1940 July 19 | Hank Leiber | Dodgers—Wyatt | 1 | H |
| 1940 Sept. 7 | Bill Nicholson | Reds—Derringer | 4 | H |
| 1941 May 19 | Claude Passeau | Dodgers—Casey | 2 | H |
| 1941 May 21 | Bill Nicholson | Phillies—Hoerst | 5 | H |
| 1941 June 10 | Hank Leiber | Giants—McGee | 1 | A |
| 1941 July 5 | Dom Dallessandro | Pirates—Sullivan | 7 | A |
| 1941 July 29 | Bill Nicholson | Phillies—Melton | 8 | H |
| 1941 Aug. 26 | Dom Dallessandro | Phillies—Beck | 4 | A |
| *1941 Sept. 20 | Bob Scheffing | Cardinals—Krist | 9 | A |
| 1942 June 3 | Rip Russell | Giants—Sunkel | 1 | H |
| *1942 June 21 | Dom Dallessandro | Giants—McGee | 9 | A |
| 1944 June 28 | Bill Nicholson | Dodgers—Webber | 6 | H |
| 1944 Aug. 16 | Bill Nicholson | Braves—Rich | 3 | H |
| 1944 Aug. 20 | Len Merullo | Giants—Feldman | 4 | H |
| 1945 Aug. 15 | Paul Gillespie | Dodgers—Herring | 1 | A |
| 1945 Sept. 3 | Andy Pafko | Reds—Heusser | 1 | H |
| 1945 Sept. 23 | Andy Pafko | Pirates—Roe | 3 | H |
| *1946 June 6 | Frank Secory | Giants—Koslo | 12 | H |
| 1946 Sept. 16 | Bill Nicholson | Dodgers—Minner | 7 | A |
| 1947 Apr. 20 | Bill Nicholson | Cardinals—Pollet | 5 | A |
| 1947 Aug. 24 | Eddie Waitkus | Giants—Iott | 5 | A |
| 1947 Sept. 8 | John Miller | Pirates—Higbe | 2 | A |
| *1947 Sept. 9 | Cliff Aberson | Dodgers—Lombardi | 8 | H |
| 1949 Sept. 4 | Andy Pafko | Pirates—Sewell | 4 | H |
| 1949 Sept. 9 | Andy Pafko | Pirates—Poat | 5 | A |

*Pinch-hitter

# (1950–1959)

| Date | Player | Team Pitcher | Inning | Site |
|------|--------|--------------|--------|------|
| 1950 May 18 | Rube Walker | Giants—Hartung | 6 | A |
| 1950 May 26 | Roy Smalley | Pirates—Queen | 4 | A |
| *1950 Sept. 18 | Ron Northey | Dodgers—Bankhead | 7 | A |
| 1951 May 3 | Andy Pafko | Braves—Surkont | 6 | A |
| 1951 May 18 | Jack Cusick | Phillies—Johnson | 4 | H |
| *1951 July 29 | Phil Cavarretta | Phillies—Roberts | 7 | H |
| 1951 Aug. 18 | Randy Jackson | Pirates—Pollet | 1 | A |
| 1952 Apr. 15 | Hank Sauer | Reds—Wehmeier | 3 | A |
| 1952 July 22 | Dee Fondy | Braves—Bickford | 4 | A |
| 1953 June 14 | Ralph Kiner | Dodgers—Erskine | 9 | A |
| 1953 June 19 | Randy Jackson | Dodgers—Loes | 5 | H |
| *1953 Aug. 14 | Bill Serena | Braves—Jolly | 6 | H |
| 1954 May 17 | Hank Sauer | Pirates—Purkey | 5 | A |
| 1954 May 29 | Walker Cooper | Reds—Baczewski | 4 | H |
| 1954 July 18 | Walker Cooper | Dodgers—Meyer | 4 | H |
| 1954 Aug. 17 | Clyde McCullough | Reds—Podbelian | 4 | H |
| 1955 May 11 | Ernie Banks | Dodgers—Meyer | 1 | H |
| 1955 May 29 | Ernie Banks | Braves—Burdette | 3 | H |
| 1955 July 1 | Gene Baker | Cardinals—Lawrence | 2 | H |
| 1955 July 17 | Ernie Banks | Phillies—Negray | 6 | A |
| 1955 Aug. 2 | Ernie Banks | Pirates—Littlefield | 5 | H |
| 1955 Sept. 19 | Ernie Banks | Cardinals—McDaniel | 7 | A |
| 1956 July 8 | Monte Irvin | Braves—Conley | 9 | A |
| 1956 July 15 | Gene Baker | Dodgers—Newcombe | 3 | H |
| 1956 Aug. 23 | Gene Baker | Giants—Surkont | 7 | H |
| 1957 Apr. 30 | Moose Moryn | Dodgers—Labine | 7 | A |
| *1959 May 12 | Earl Averill | Braves—Burdette | 9 | H |
| 1959 May 13 | Ernie Banks | Reds—Purkey | 3 | H |
| 1959 July 22 | Earl Averill | Dodgers—McDevitt | 2 | A |
| 1959 Aug. 13 | Al Dark | Giants—McCormick | 7 | H |
| 1959 Aug. 29 | Ernie Banks | Braves—Spahn | 3 | H |

*Pinch-hitter

♦

# (1960–1969)

| Date | | Player | Team Pitcher | Inning | Site |
|---|---|---|---|---|---|
| 1960 | Apr. 14 | Ernie Banks | Giants—Sanford | 3 | A |
| 1960 | Aug. 14 | Ron Santo | Phillies—Green | 6 | A |
| 1961 | Apr. 15 | Al Heist | Braves—Nottebart | 9 | H |
| 1961 | May 2 | Billy Williams | Giants—Fisher | 2 | H |
| 1961 | May 28 | Ernie Banks | Giants—Miller | 8 | H |
| 1961 | June 16 | Billy Williams | Giants—Jones | 3 | A |
| 1962 | May 20 | Lou Brock | Phillies—Owens | 2 | A |
| 1962 | Sept. 16 | Nellie Mathews | Dodgers—Williams | 1 | H |
| 1963 | Aug. 31 | Ellis Burton | Colts—Woodeshick | 9 | H |
| 1963 | Sept. 2 | Ron Santo | Giants—Fisher | 5 | H |
| 1964 | June 12 | Joe Amalfitano | Pirates—Face | 6 | H |
| 1964 | May 1 | Billy Williams | Colts—Hoerner | 1 | A |
| 1964 | Sept. 27 | Ernie Banks | Giants—Bolin | 5 | H |
| 1965 | July 20 | Ed Bailey | Phillies—Wagner | 5 | H |
| 1965 | Aug. 27 | Billy Williams | Braves—Johnson | 5 | A |
| 1966 | June 8 | Randy Hundley | Dodgers—Drysdale | 4 | H |
| 1967 | May 20 | Randy Hundley | Dodgers—Lee | 7 | H |
| 1967 | July 13 | Adolfo Phillips | Giants—Perry | 6 | A |
| 1968 | July 7 | Ernie Banks | Pirates—Blass | 1 | H |
| 1968 | July 14 | Billy Williams | Pirates—McBean | 7 | A |
| 1968 | Sept. 25 | Ron Santo | Dodgers—Singer | 9 | H |
| 1969 | May 24 | Ernie Banks | Padres—Baldschun | 5 | A |
| 1969 | May 28 | Randy Hundley | Giants—Sadecki | 3 | A |
| 1969 | Aug. 23 | Jim Hickman | Astros—Gladding | 7 | H |

# (1970–1979)

| Date | Player | Team Pitcher | Inning | Site |
|---|---|---|---|---|
| 1970 Apr. 26 | Ron Santo | Astros—Dierker | 6 | H |
| 1970 July 3 | Billy Williams | Pirates—Gibbon | 2 | H |
| 1970 July 6 | Ron Santo | Expos—Wegener | 1 | H |
| 1970 Aug. 14 | Joe Pepitone | Dodgers—Sutton | 1 | H |
| 1971 Aug. 18 | Johnny Callison | Braves—Niekro | 8 | A |
| 1971 Sept. 11 | Paul Popovich | Cardinals—Reuss | 3 | H |
| 1972 June 20 | Randy Hundley | Giants—Carrithers | 1 | H |
| 1972 Sept. 15 | Jim Hickman | Mets—Gentry | 3 | H |
| 1972 Sept. 16 | Burt Hooton | Mets—Seaver | 3 | H |
| 1972 Sept. 27 | Billy Williams | Expos—Renko | 5 | A |
| 1973 July 6 | Rick Monday | Padres—Kirby | 5 | A |
| 1974 Apr. 17 | George Mitterwald | Pirates—Reuss | 1 | H |
| 1974 July 26 | Billy Williams | Phillies—Hernaiz | 6 | H |
| 1974 Aug. 20 | Carmen Fanzone | Dodgers—Hough | 8 | H |
| *1974 Aug. 28 | Bill Madlock | Dodgers—Sutton | 8 | A |
| 1974 Sept. 8 | Jerry Morales | Phillies—Christenson | 9 | H |
| 1974 Sept. 21 | Steve Swisher | Cardinals—Lersch | 6 | A |
| *1975 Aug. 23 | Champ Summers | Astros—York | 7 | H |
| *1975 Sept. 3 | Pete LaCock | Cardinals—Gibson | 7 | A |
| *1975 Sept. 14 | Tim Hosley | Phillies—Lerch | 9 | H |
| 1976 June 18 | Bill Madlock | Braves—Leon | 7 | A |
| 1978 Apr. 26 | Bobby Murcer | Phillies—Carlton | 3 | A |
| 1978 June 3 | Dave Kingman | Astros—Zamora | 6 | H |
| *1978 June 26 | Dave Rader | Mets—Murray | 5 | H |
| 1979 Apr. 20 | Dave Kingman | Expos—Rogers | 3 | H |
| 1979 May 15 | Barry Foote | Phillies—Espinosa | 5 | H |
| 1979 May 17 | Bill Buckner | Phillies—McGraw | 5 | H |
| *1979 June 30 | Mike Vail | Mets—Murray | 11 | H |
| 1979 Sept. 9 | Barry Foote | Phillies—Kucek | 4 | H |

*Pinch-hitter

# (1980–1990)

| Date | Player | Team Pitcher | Inning | Site |
|---|---|---|---|---|
| 1980 Apr. 19 | Dave Kingman | Mets—Allen | 8 | H |
| 1980 Apr. 22 | Barry Foote | Cardinals—Littell | 9 | H |
| 1980 June 22 | Jerry Martin | Reds—Bair | 7 | H |
| 1980 July 12 | Cliff Johnson | Expos—Bahnsen | 7–2dG | A |
| 1980 Aug. 8 | Cliff Johnson | Expos—Murray | 14 | H |
| 1983 May 31 | Ryne Sandberg | Astros—LaCorte | 6 | H |
| 1983 June 12 | Jody Davis | Cardinals—Forsch | 4 | H |
| 1983 June 26 | Jody Davis | Expos—Lerch | 2 | A |
| 1983 Aug. 11 | Leon Durham | Cardinals—Cox | 3 | H |
| 1983 Aug. 29 | Mel Hall | Braves—P. Niekro | 5 | A |
| 1984 May 8 | Ron Cey | Giants—Garrelts | 3 | H |
| 1984 Aug. 5 | Keith Moreland | Expos—Grapethin | 3 | H |
| 1984 Sept. 14 | Jody Davis | Mets—Gaff | 6 | H |
| 1985 May 22 | Brian Dayett | Reds—Browning | 6 | H |
| 1985 June 11 | Leon Durham | Expos—Lucas | 8 | A |
| 1985 Aug. 14 | Ron Cey | Expos—Smith | 3 | H |
| 1986 Apr. 27 | Jody Davis | Expos—McGaffigan | 4 | H |
| 1987 Apr. 22 | Andre Dawson | Cardinals—Worrell | 7 | A |
| 1987 June 1 | Andre Dawson | Astros—Solano | 8 | H |
| 1987 June 3 | Brian Dayett | Astros—Knepper | 1 | H |
| 1987 June 3 | Keith Moreland | Astros—Solano | 6 | H |
| 1987 July 8 | Jim Sundberg | Padres—McCullers | 8 | H |
| 1987 Aug. 18 | Jody Davis | Mets—Darling | 4 | H |
| 1988 Apr. 8 | Davey Martinez | Expos—Youmans | 2 | A |
| 1988 Sept. 13 | Damon Berryhill | Phillies—Barojas | 7 | A |
| 1988 Oct. 1 | Rafael Palmeiro | Pirates—Kipper | 5 | H |
| *1989 July 31 | Dwight Smith | Phillies—Harris | 7 | A |
| 1989 Sept. 15 | Shawon Dunston | Pirates—Patterson | 6 | A |

*Pinch-hitter

# Two–Home Run Games by Chicago Cubs

| George Altman | E. Banks (cont.) | Vince Barton |
|---|---|---|
| 8/13/59 | 4/30/58 | 8/4/31 |
| 9/21/59 | 5/28/58 | |
| 7/6/60 | 6/4/58 | **Clyde Beck** |
| 8/4/61 | 7/1/58 | 5/12/30 |
| 5/15/62 | 8/16/58 | |
| 5/18/62 | 8/21/58 | **Glenn Beckert** |
| 5/22/66 | 4/14/59 | 7/1/65 |
| | 7/29/59 | |
| **Adrian Anson** | 4/29/60 | **Damon Berryhill** |
| 7/9/1884 | 6/21/60 | 8/22/88 |
| 8/5/1884 | 5/3/61 | |
| 9/4/1885 | 5/9/61 | **Larry Biittner** |
| 8/24/1886 | 7/28/61 | 5/17/77 |
| 7/28/1888 | 8/17/61 | |
| 10/3/1897 | 7/25/62 | **John Boccabella** |
| | 5/1/63 | 9/12/65 |
| **Maurice Atwell** | 6/5/63 | |
| 7/4/52 | 5/9/65 | **Bobby Bonds** |
| | 8/27/65 | 9/7/81 |
| **Ed Bailey** | 5/20/66 | 9/9/81 |
| 7/22/65 | 6/25/67 | |
| | 5/26/68 | **Thad Bosley** |
| **Ernie Banks** | 6/10/68 | 8/12/85 |
| 8/22/54 | 7/17/68 | |
| 4/16/55 | 7/31/68 | **Lou Brock** |
| 6/28/55 | 8/26/68 | 7/28/63 |
| 7/8/55 | 4/8/69 | |
| 7/1/56 | 6/13/69 | **Jonathan Brooks** |
| 7/20/57 | 8/24/69 | 6/8/25 |
| 9/2/57 | 6/29/70 | 6/15/25 |
| 9/10/57 | | |

♦

**Byron Browne**
7/18/66

**Bill Buckner**
7/28/77
8/19/77
5/1/79
9/27/81 (2)
8/9/82
5/30/83

**Thomas E. Burns**
7/4/1884
6/13/1885
10/6/1885

**Ellis Burton**
8/1/63
9/7/64

**Jose Cardenal**
5/24/72
9/16/72

**Don Cardwell**
9/2/60

**Phil Cavarretta**
8/30/36

**Ron Cey**
7/30/83 (2)
9/15/83
7/5/84
5/26/85
9/28/85
5/3/86

**Harry Chiti**
8/29/55

**John Clarkson**
10/9/1884
8/13/1887

**Rip Collins**
5/2/38

**Hector Cruz**
4/28/78

**Kiki Cuyler**
6/18/28
7/1/30

**Babe Dahlgren**
6/19/41

**Dom Dallessandro**
7/28/42

**Abner Dalrymple**
8/14/1884

**Thomas Daly**
5/20/1887

**Jody Davis**
5/11/82
5/27/83
9/23/83
6/12/84
8/9/85
4/27/86
5/16/86
5/6/87
5/27/88

**Andre Dawson**
4/26/87
6/1/87
6/2/87
7/6/87
8/6/87
8/20/87
8/21/87
4/29/88
5/3/88
8/19/88

**A. Dawson** (cont.)
5/5/89
9/3/89
9/25/89

**Brian Dayett**
5/17/87

**George Decker**
9/16/1894

**Frank Demaree**
4/14/36
6/14/36
7/26/36
9/8/38

**Steve Dillard**
8/9/79

**Hugh Duffy**
8/9/1889

**Shawon Dunston**
6/4/89

**Leon Durham**
8/26/81
6/28/82
8/15/82 (2)
5/24/84 (1)
8/26/84
7/7/85
8/29/85
5/9/87
8/27/87 (2)
9/6/87

**Howard Earl**
9/12/1890

**Henry Edwards**
6/30/49

◆
**161**

**Elwood English**
6/7/30

**William Everett**
8/30/1897

**Carmen Fanzone**
5/6/72

**Frank Flint**
7/24/1882

**Dee Fondy**
5/16/51
6/9/53
4/16/55
7/27/55

**Barry Foote**
7/10/79
4/22/80

**Elmer Foster**
9/5/1890

**Bernard Friberg**
4/20/23

**Augie Galan**
6/11/35
9/4/35
6/25/37

**Paul Gillespie**
8/15/45

**Fred Goldsmith**
5/27/1884

**George Gore**
9/16/1884
6/6/1885

**Mark Grace**
8/19/89

**George
   Grantham**
9/23/24

**Charles Grimm**
6/13/25
5/7/29

**Stan Hack**
9/14/40
9/18/40
6/11/41

**Mel Hall**
7/11/83
8/29/83
8/31/83
9/10/83

**Gabby Hartnett**
4/20/23
7/20/24
7/22/24
4/16/25
7/2/25
8/24/26
4/28/30
6/13/30
6/25/30
9/4/30
9/27/30
5/2/33
4/29/34
9/10/37

**Tully Hartsel**
8/5/01

**Cliff Heathcote**
6/1/26
5/12/30

**Steve Henderson**
5/25/81

**Elrod Hendricks**
9/1/72

**Babe Herman**
7/29/33
8/12/34

**James Hickman**
8/9/69
8/23/69
5/28/70
8/19/70
4/28/72

**Glen Hobbie**
7/2/61

**Rogers Hornsby**
6/30/31

**Randy Hundley**
8/9/66
6/11/67

**Monte Irvin**
7/20/56

**Charles Irwin**
6/11/1894

**Darrin Jackson**
9/17/88

**Ransom Jackson**
5/16/51
7/13/51
7/3/53
7/5/54
7/22/54
4/16/55

**Hal Jeffcoat**
8/26/53

**Ferguson Jenkins**
9/1/71

**Jay Johnstone**
8/8/82

**Tony Kaufmann**
7/4/25

**Mike Kelly**
9/23/1885
9/25/1885

**Jerry Kindall**
7/12/57

**Ralph Kiner**
6/7/53
7/5/53
7/12/53
6/8/54

**James King**
6/28/55
7/4/56
8/21/56

**Dave Kingman**
6/1/79
7/27/79
4/11/80
4/19/80
8/26/80
9/14/80

**Chuck Klein**
5/17/34
6/12/35
6/17/35
4/19/36

**Vance Law**
7/29/88
7/22/89

**Bill Lee**
5/7/41

**Hank Leiber**
9/13/39
7/21/40
6/18/41

**Dale Long**
7/4/57

**Clarence Maddern**
5/21/48

**Bill Madlock**
9/24/74

**Jim Marshall**
8/24/58
5/7/59

**Jerry Martin**
6/2/79
4/11/80
8/5/80

**Gary Matthews**
7/11/86
9/10/86

**Sam Mertes**
9/24/1899
6/8/00

**Lawrence Miller**
7/14/22
8/25/22
6/12/23

**George Mitterwald**
7/28/77

**Rick Monday**
7/11/72
6/10/73
6/28/73
7/3/73
9/9/73
9/24/74
4/17/76
5/5/76
9/3/76

**Jerry Morales**
5/22/74
4/13/76

**Keith Moreland**
5/7/82
6/17/84
7/17/84
9/28/85
9/9/86
6/3/87

**Walt Moryn**
4/27/56
5/31/56
9/3/56
6/19/57
5/2/58
6/19/58
9/7/58

**Joe Munson**
5/1/26

**Bobby Murcer**
8/8/77
8/17/77
5/28/79

**Dan Murphy**
9/27/61

**Bill Nicholson**
6/6/40
8/15/42
5/30/43
6/20/43
9/23/43
6/18/44
6/28/44
7/4/45
4/20/47
8/16/47
8/28/47
9/6/47

**Bob O'Farrell**
6/14/23

**Andy Pafko**
5/16/48
5/7/49
6/19/49
4/18/50
7/28/50
4/22/51
5/11/51

**Rafael Palmeiro**
5/28/88

**Fred Pfeffer**
8/12/1884
9/24/1884

**Adolfo Phillips**
7/30/68

**James Ryan**
8/25/1891
6/5/1896
7/11/1899

**Vic Saier**
7/2/14

**Ryne Sandberg**
4/23/82
6/1/84
6/23/84
7/9/85
7/14/85
8/21/85
5/30/86
6/1/88
6/4/89
7/31/89 (1)
8/10/89
8/20/89
9/8/89

**Ron Santo**
8/18/60
6/28/61
8/27/61
8/4/63
9/2/63
6/18/64
7/1/64
4/14/65
8/29/65
9/21/65
4/28/66
6/4/66
6/18/66
8/5/66
7/1/67
4/25/68
8/30/68
4/10/69
8/2/69
7/6/70
9/7/70
5/20/71
8/26/72
4/24/73

**R. Santo** (cont.)
6/27/73

**Hank Sauer**
7/20/49
9/3/49
5/27/50
6/25/50
8/24/50
8/25/50
7/14/51
8/14/51
9/5/51
8/11/52
8/21/52
5/2/54
5/31/54
6/5/54
7/17/54
8/17/55

**Frank Schulte**
8/26/10
8/28/10
8/12/11
9/7/13

**Frank Secory**
9/16/44

**Bill Serena**
6/6/50
7/18/50
5/27/52

**Jimmy Sheckard**
8/28/10

**Willie Smith**
8/20/68

**Al Spangler**
6/12/69

**Chris Speier**
6/6/86

**Riggs Stephenson**
6/14/26
7/1/29

**Scott Stratton**
7/27/1894

**Tony Taylor**
7/1/58

**Sam Taylor**
6/27/61
7/2/61

**Frank Thomas**
5/3/60
6/5/60

**Bobby Thomson**
6/10/58
8/17/58
5/10/59

**Mike Vail**
5/6/79

**Lee Walls**
7/19/57
8/12/58
4/29/58

**Earl Webb**
4/12/27

**Pete Whisenant**
5/12/56

**Billy Williams**
7/14/61
8/2/61
5/5/62
6/20/63
8/23/63
4/17/64
6/17/64
9/5/65
7/26/66
6/1/67
6/5/67
7/22/67
9/29/67
4/11/68
7/21/68
8/11/68
9/8/68
9/5/69
5/8/70
5/23/70
7/4/70
5/1/71
5/19/71
8/8/71
9/29/71
6/15/72
8/26/72
6/1/73

**Cy Williams**
7/10/15
9/2/16

**Ed Williamson**
6/24/1884
10/4/1884

**Walter Wilmot**
6/28/1890

**W. Wilmot** (cont.)
9/17/1890
6/8/1891
8/25/1891
7/4/1895

**Hack Wilson**
8/16/26
8/24/27
9/7/27
4/19/28
5/21/28
6/30/28
7/6/28
8/6/28
8/25/28
4/28/29
6/4/29
6/18/29
6/20/29
7/11/29
7/24/29
7/31/29
5/18/30
6/1/30
7/21/30
8/10/30
8/30/30
9/17/30
9/27/30

**Don Zimmer**
7/23/61

**Henry Zimmerman**
10/3/10
6/11/11
6/10/12
8/16/13
5/12/16

◆
**165**

# Three–Home Run Games by Chicago Cubs

| Player | Date | Team | Site |
|---|---|---|---|
| Ed Williamson | May 30, 1884 | Buffalo | Chicago (Michigan & Randolph) |
| *Cap Anson | Aug. 6, 1884 | Cleveland | Chicago (Michigan & Randolph) |
| Hack Wilson | July 26, 1930 | Pirates | Forbes Field |
| *Rogers Hornsby | Apr. 24, 1931 | Phillies | Baker Bowl |
| Babe Herman | July 20, 1933 | Phillies | Wrigley Field |
| *Hank Leiber | July 4, 1939 | Cardinals | Wrigley Field |
| *Clyde McCullough | July 26, 1942 | Braves | Braves Field |
| *Bill Nicholson | July 23, 1944 | Giants | Polo Grounds |
| *Andy Pafko | Aug. 2, 1950 | Giants | Polo Grounds |
| *Hank Sauer | Aug. 28, 1950 | Phillies | Wrigley Field |
| Hank Sauer | June 11, 1952 | Phillies | Wrigley Field |
| Ernie Banks | Aug. 4, 1955 | Pirates | Wrigley Field |
| *Ernie Banks | Sept. 14, 1957 | Pirates | Wrigley Field |
| Lee Walls | Apr. 24, 1958 | Dodgers | LA Coliseum |
| Moose Moryn | May 30, 1958 | Dodgers | Wrigley Field |
| Ernie Banks | May 29, 1962 | Braves | Wrigley Field |
| Ernie Banks | June 9, 1963 | Dodgers | Wrigley Field |
| Adolfo Phillips | June 11, 1967 | Mets | Wrigley Field |
| Billy Williams | Sept. 10, 1968 | Mets | Wrigley Field |
| *Rick Monday | May 16, 1972 | Phillies | Veterans Stadium |
| George Mitterwald | Apr. 17, 1974 | Pirates | Wrigley Field |
| Dave Kingman | May 14, 1978 | Dodgers | Dodger Stadium (15 innings) |
| Dave Kingman | May 17, 1979 | Phillies | Wrigley Field |
| *Dave Kingman | July 28, 1979 | Mets | Shea Stadium |
| Andre Dawson | Aug. 1, 1987 | Phillies | Wrigley Field |

*Consecutive homers

♦

# Homers In One Inning

## Four

| Players | Inning | Date |
|---|---|---|
| (Heathcote, Wilson, Grimm, Beck) | 7th | May 12, 1930 |

## Three

| Players | Inning | Date |
|---|---|---|
| (Hornsby, Wilson, Grimm) | 5th | June 4, 1929 |
| (Wilson, Malone, Hornsby) | 2d | June 28, 1929 |
| (Collins, Marty, Bottarini) | 8th | May 4, 1937 |
| (Nicholson, Russell, French) | 3d | Sept. 6, 1939 |
| *(Cavarretta, Hack, Nicholson) | 5th | Aug. 11, 1941 |
| (Dallessandro, Nicholson, Johnson) | 6th | June 27, 1947 |
| (Ramazzotti, Cavarretta, Borkowski) | 6th | June 13, 1950 |
| (Minner, Jackson, Serena) | 4th | May 31, 1954 |
| *(Jackson, Banks, Fondy) | 2d | Apr. 16, 1955 |
| (Sauer, Jackson, Baker) | 2d | July 1, 1955 |
| (Chiti, Fondy, Baker) | 4th | Aug. 29, 1955 |
| (Fondy, Banks, Miksis) | 1st | Sept. 9, 1955 (1st game) |
| (Fondy, Baker, Banks) | 8th | Sept. 9, 1955 (2d game) |
| (Zimmer, Santo, Altman) | 6th | Sept. 18, 1960 |
| (Williams, Santo, Cowan) | 4th | June 2, 1964 |
| (Williams, Santo, Hundley) | 1st | July 3, 1967 |
| (Williams, Banks, Hickman) | 4th | July 31, 1968 |
| (Pepitone, Callison, Beckert) | 8th | Aug. 19, 1970 |
| (Williams, Santo, Cardenal) | 4th | May 1, 1973 |
| (Monday, Bourque, Santo) | 1st | June 10, 1973 |

♦

| Players | Inning | Date |
|---|---|---|
| (Biittner, Ontiveros, Clines) | 3d | May 17, 1977 |
| *(Biittner, Murcer, Morales) | 5th | May 17, 1977 |
| (Dunston, Webster, Sandberg) | 5th | June 4, 1989 |

*Consecutive homers

# All-Star Game Homers

| Year | Player | Inning | Pitcher | Site |
|------|--------|--------|---------|------|
| 1936 | Augie Galan | 5 | Rowe | Braves Field |
| 1952 | Hank Sauer | 4 | Lemon | Shibe Park |
| 1960 | Ernie Banks | 1 | Monbouquette | KC Municipal Stadium |
| 1961 | George Altman | 8 | Bunning | Candlestick Park |
| 1964 | Billy Williams | 4 | Wyatt | Shea Stadium |

# NL Championship Playoff Homers

| Date | Player | Inning | Players On Base | Site |
|---|---|---|---|---|
| Oct. 2, 1984 | Bob Dernier | 1 | 0 | Wrigley Field |
| Oct. 2, 1984 | Gary Matthews | 1 | 0 | Wrigley Field |
| Oct. 2, 1984 | Rick Sutcliffe | 3 | 0 | Wrigley Field |
| Oct. 2, 1984 | Gary Matthews | 5 | 2 | Wrigley Field |
| Oct. 2, 1984 | Ron Cey | 6 | 0 | Wrigley Field |
| Oct. 6, 1984 | Jody Davis | 4 | 1 | Jack Murphy Stadium |
| Oct. 6, 1984 | Leon Durham | 4 | 0 | Jack Murphy Stadium |
| Oct. 7, 1984 | Leon Durham | 1 | 1 | Jack Murphy Stadium |
| Oct. 7, 1984 | Jody Davis | 2 | 0 | Jack Murphy Stadium |
| Oct. 4, 1989 | Mark Grace | 1 | 1 | Wrigley Field |
| Oct. 4, 1989 | Ryne Sandberg | 3 | 0 | Wrigley Field |
| Oct. 8, 1989 | Luis Salazar | 2 | 0 | Candlestick Park |

# World Series Homers

| Year | Player | Game | Inning | Pitcher | Team | Site |
|------|--------|------|--------|---------|------|------|
| 1908 | Joe Tinker | 2 | 8 | Donovan | Tigers | H |
| 1929 | Charlie Grimm | 4 | 4 | Quinn | Athletics | A |
| 1932 | Kiki Cuyler | 3 | 3 | Pipgras | Yankees | H |
| 1932 | Gabby Hartnett | 3 | 9 | Pipgras | Yankees | H |
| 1932 | Frank Demaree | 4 | 1 | Allen | Yankees | H |
| 1935 | Frank Demaree | 1 | 9 | Rowe | Tigers | A |
| 1935 | Frank Demaree | 3 | 2 | Aucker | Tigers | H |
| 1935 | Gabby Hartnett | 4 | 2 | Crowder | Tigers | H |
| 1935 | Chuck Klein | 5 | 3 | Rowe | Tigers | H |
| 1935 | Billy Herman | 6 | 5 | Bridges | Tigers | A |
| 1938 | Joe Marty | 3 | 8 | Pearson | Yankees | A |
| 1938 | Ken O'Dea | 4 | 8 | Ruffing | Yankees | A |
| 1945 | Phil Cavarretta | 1 | 7 | Tobin | Tigers | A |

◆

# Home Run Leaders By Position (Lifetime)

## Modern

| Position | Player | Years | Total |
|---|---|---|---|
| 1B | Ernie Banks | (1961–1971) | 214 |
| 2B | Ryne Sandberg | (1982–1989) | 139 |
| SS | Ernie Banks | (1953–1961) | 298 |
| 3B | Ron Santo | (1960–1973) | 337 |
| OF | Billy Williams | (1959–1974) | 392 |
| OF | Bill Nicholson | (1939–1948) | 205 |
| OF | Hank Sauer | (1949–1955) | 198 |
| C | Gabby Hartnett | (1922–1940) | 231 |
| P | Fergie Jenkins | (1966–1973, 1982–1983) | 13 |

## 19th Century

| Position | Player | Years | Total |
|---|---|---|---|
| 1B | Cap Anson | (1876–1897) | 97 |
| 2B | Fred Pfeffer | (1883–1889, 1896–1897) | 79 |
| SS | Bill Dahlen | (1891–1898) | 57 |
| 3B | Ed Williamson | (1879–1889) | 61 |
| OF | Jimmy Ryan | (1885–1900) | 99 |
| OF | Walt Wilmot | (1890–1895) | 43 |
| OF | Bill Lange | (1893–1899) | 40 |
| C | King Kelly | (1880–1886) | 33 |
| P | John Clarkson | (1884–1887) | 16 |

◆

# All-Time

| Position | Player | Years | Total |
|----------|--------|-------|-------|
| 1B | Ernie Banks | (1961–1971) | 214 |
| 2B | Ryne Sandberg | (1982–1989) | 139 |
| SS | Ernie Banks | (1953–1961) | 298 |
| 3B | Ron Santo | (1960–1973) | 337 |
| OF | Billy Williams | (1959–1974) | 392 |
| OF | Bill Nicholson | (1939–1948) | 205 |
| OF | Hank Sauer | (1949–1955) | 198 |
| C | Gabby Hartnett | (1922–1940) | 231 |
| P | John Clarkson | (1884–1887) | 16 |

# Home Run Leaders By Position (Season)

## Modern

| Position | Player | Years | Total |
|----------|--------|-------|-------|
| 1B | Ernie Banks | 1962 | 37 |
| 2B | Rogers Hornsby | 1929 | 39 |
| SS | Ernie Banks | 1958 | 47 |
| 3B | Ron Santo | 1965 | 33 |
| CF | Hack Wilson | 1930 | 56 |
| LF | Dave Kingman | 1979 | 48 |
| RF | Andre Dawson | 1987 | 49 |
| C | Gabby Hartnett | 1930 | 37 |
| P | Fergie Jenkins | 1971 | 6 |

## 19th Century

| Position | Player | Years | Total |
|----------|--------|-------|-------|
| 1B | Cap Anson | 1884 | 21 |
| 2B | Fred Pfeffer | 1884 | 25 |
| SS | Bill Dahlen | 1894 | 15 |
| 3B | Ed Williamson | 1884 | 27 |
| OF | Abner Dalrymple | 1884 | 22 |
| OF | Jimmy Ryan | 1889 | 17 |
| OF | Walt Wilmot | 1890 | 14 |
| C | King Kelly | 1884 | 13 |
| P | Addison Gumbert | 1889 | 7 |

◆

# All-Time

| Position | Player | Years | Total |
|----------|--------|-------|-------|
| 1B | Ernie Banks | 1962 | 37 |
| 2B | Rogers Hornsby | 1929 | 39 |
| SS | Ernie Banks | 1958 | 47 |
| 3B | Ron Santo | 1965 | 33 |
| CF | Hack Wilson | 1930 | 56 |
| LF | Dave Kingman | 1979 | 48 |
| RF | Andre Dawson | 1987 | 49 |
| C | Gabby Hartnett | 1930 | 37 |
| P | Addison Gumbert | 1889 | 7 |

♦

# Home Run Frequency

| Player | At Bats | Homers | Frequency |
|--------|---------|--------|-----------|
| Dave Kingman | 1182 | 94 | 12.6 |
| Hank Sauer | 3165 | 198 | 15.9 |
| Hack Wilson | 3154 | 190 | 16.6 |
| Andre Dawson | 1628 | 95 | 17.1 |
| Ernie Banks | 9421 | 512 | 18.4 |
| Rogers Hornsby | 1121 | 58 | 19.3 |
| Ralph Kiner | 971 | 50 | 19.4 |
| Jim Hickman | 1992 | 97 | 20.5 |
| Dale Long | 1173 | 55 | 21.3 |
| Billy Williams | 8479 | 392 | 21.6 |
| Ron Cey | 1842 | 84 | 21.8 |
| Ron Santo | 7768 | 337 | 23.0 |
| Leon Durham | 3215 | 138 | 23.2 |
| Bill Nicholson | 4857 | 205 | 23.7 |
| Rick Monday | 2551 | 106 | 24.1 |
| Walt Moryn | 2099 | 84 | 24.9 |
| George Altman | 2205 | 83 | 26.6 |
| Gabby Hartnett | 6282 | 231 | 27.2 |
| Jody Davis | 3318 | 122 | 27.2 |
| Andy Pafko | 3567 | 126 | 28.3 |
| Randy Jackson | 2602 | 88 | 29.6 |

# A Chronology of Cubs Player Transactions 1985–1990

How the NL East champion Cubs of 1984 evolved into the division champions of 1989 (with some forgettable seasons in between) can be seen in the player transaction listing carried below in chronological order. It is a time capsule reflection of the changing face of our favorite team.

As can be seen, a great deal can occur over a relatively short period of time. Five years ago, fans thought the glory of the 1984 Cubs would last forever; yet, the only veterans of that team still with the Cubs are Ryne Sandberg and Rick Sutcliffe. Here is what happened in between.


**April 5, 1985**—Utility infielder Tom Veryzer released

**August 13, 1985**—Shortstop Larry Bowa released

**December 11, 1985**—Infielder Dave Owen traded to Giants for former Cub second baseman Manny Trillo and cash

**December 16, 1985**—Outfielder Billy Hatcher traded to Astros for outfielder Jerry Mumphrey

♦

**March 31, 1986**—Outfielder Gary Woods released

**April 1, 1986**—Infielder Richie Hebner released

**April 7, 1986**—Pitcher Warren Brusstar released

**May 6, 1986**—Pitcher Dick Ruthven released

**June 12, 1986**—Manager Jim Frey and coach Don Zimmer fired

**June 14, 1986**—Gene Michael hired as manager

**July 21, 1986**—Infielder Davey Lopes traded to Astros for pitcher Frank DiPino

**August 13, 1986**—Pitchers Ray Fontenot and George Frazier traded to Twins for pitcher Ron Davis

**January 30, 1987**—Third baseman Ron Cey traded to Athletics for infielder Luis Quinones

**March 6, 1987**—Outfielder Andre Dawson signed as free agent

**March 30, 1987**—Outfielder Thad Bosley and pitcher Dave Gumpert traded to Royals for catcher Jim Sundberg

**April 3, 1987**—Pitcher Dennis Eckersley traded to Athletics for outfielder Dave Wilder, infielder Brian Guinn, and pitcher Mark Leonette

**July 11, 1987**—Outfielder Gary Matthews traded to Mariners for pitcher Dave Hartnett

◆

**July 13, 1987**—Pitcher Steve Trout traded to Yankees for pitchers Bob Tewksbury, Rick Scheid, and Dean Williams

**August 4, 1987**—Pitcher Ron Davis released

**September 8, 1987**—Gene Michael resigns as manager; Frank Lucchesi becomes interim manager

**October 16, 1987**—Outfielder Chico Walker traded to Angels for pitcher Todd Fischer

**October 27, 1987**—Outfielder Bobby Dernier files for free agency; he later signs with the Phillies

**November 20, 1987**—Don Zimmer named Cub manager

**December 8, 1987**—Lee Smith traded to Red Sox for pitchers Al Nipper and Calvin Schiraldi

**December 14, 1987**—Third baseman Vance Law signed as free agent

**February 12, 1988**—Infielders Keith Moreland and Mike Brumley traded to Padres for pitchers Rich Gossage and Ray Hayward

**March 21, 1988**—Pitcher Paul Mason released

**March 28, 1988**—Pitcher Dickie Noles released

**March 31, 1988**—Pitcher Mike Curtis traded to Pirates for pitcher Mike Bielecki

**April 1, 1988**—Infielder Luis Quinones traded to Reds for pitcher Bill Landrum

◆

**May 18, 1988**—First baseman Leon Durham traded to Reds for pitcher Pat Perry

**July 14, 1988**—Outfielder Davey Martinez traded to Expos for outfielder Mitch Webster

**July 15, 1988**—Catcher Jim Sundberg released

**September 29, 1988**—Catcher Jody Davis traded to Braves for pitchers Kevin Coffman and Kevin Blankenship

**October 15, 1988**—Pitcher Bob Tewksbury files for free agency; he later signs with the Cardinal organization

**October 26, 1988**—Infielder Manny Trillo and pitcher Frank DiPino file for free agency; Trillo later signs with the Reds and DiPino with the Cardinals

**November 10, 1988**—Outfielder Jerry Mumphrey released

**December 5, 1988**—Outfielder Rafael Palmeiro and pitchers Jamie Moyer and Drew Hall traded to Rangers for pitchers Mitch Williams, Steve Wilson and Paul Kilgus, infielders Curt Wilkerson and Luis Benetiz, and outfielder Pablo Delgado

**December 9, 1988**—Outfielder Rolando Roomes traded to Reds for outfielder Lloyd McClendon

**March 28, 1989**—Pitcher Rich Gossage released

**August 24, 1989**—Minor league pitcher Pat Gomez

and minor league catcher Kelly Mann traded to Braves for pitcher Paul Assenmacher

**August 30, 1989**—Outfielder Darrin Jackson and pitcher Calvin Schiraldi traded to Padres for outfielder Marvel Wynne, third baseman Luis Salazar, and minor league infielder Phil Stephenson

# Index